Celebrate the Temporary

Celebrate the Temporary

Johnnie J. Roebuck

The Watercress Press
San Antonio, Texas
1992

First Edition

A Watercress Press book
Published by Evett & Associates, San Antonio, Texas

Library of Congress Catalog Card No. 91-67362

ISBN 0-934955-23-9

Printed and bound in the United States of America

To my friends and to my family,
for the many wonderful temporary
celebrations.

But especially to my parents,

Marjorie Ethridge and William Leon Burns

who, through their constant faith and
positive attitudes, have taught us all what
it means to enjoy and celebrate life.

CONTENTS

Preface   viii

Foreword   ix

Stories of Family and Friends

And the Bride Wore Red   5

Surprise Celebration   10

Parents Grow Up, Too!   14

I Didn't Know I Was An Environmentalist   17

Old Shep   21

The Day Daddy Kept His Temper   27

Lessons from Mother   34

Christmas at Ma-Maw's   45

Better Than a Covered Dish   49

Time to Divide Iris—Now!   53

Stories of School and Church

Empty Eyes and Stomachs   60

The S.T.A.F.F. Meetings   64

Times Have Changed   68

A Diamond in the Rough   71

You Mean I Can't Call Them Darling?   78

Boring—Really Boring   87

Under Her Wing   90

Poetry

The Delta	95
The Lonely Steeple	96
His Spring of Life	98
I Watched My Child Fall Asleep Tonight	100
Final Requiem	102
A Fallen Flower	104
He Could Not Speak His Love	106
Little Baby, Please Don't Cry	108
Preserving Our Heritage	110
A Runner's Rage	112
Rendezvous	113
Foreign Faces	114
Sacred Shrine	116
Memories of the Sixties	118
The Birthday Resolve	120
Thank You	122

PREFACE

Johnnie Roebuck has long been known for her ability to electrify an audience when she takes the stage. Listeners find themselves moved from one strong emotion to another, from robust laughter to tears, as she weaves her stories and poems into a beautiful tapestry. Those of us who have had the pleasure of hearing Johnnie have urged her to share these gems for positive living by writing a book.

Celebrate the Temporary does just that. The insights she has given in her speeches are all here and her personality comes through vividly as she shares her inspiration for full living, every day. It is bound to put a spring in your step as she helps you celebrate life.

Let this little book lift your spirits when you are feeling low and protect you from negative thinking. Dr. Roebuck's enthusiasm is contagious. I urge you to take from her supply a helping great enough for your own needs and some to share.

Thank you, Johnnie Roebuck, for a job well done!

Ivan W. Fitzwater
August 1991

FOREWORD

Over a year ago, I was the victim of a serious automobile accident. Because of God's care, seat belts and air bags, I survived. Today, I celebrate that accident, not because it was a good experience, but because it gave me an understanding, once again, of how temporary our world is.

Until that time, I had been a healthy person, often exercising, dieting and carefully caring for my body. I can honestly say that any physical discomfort I felt was temporary and minor. I had no empathy with others who had constant aches. After the accident, I began to realize the true sense of pain. Some days my leg hurt, the next day my arm or shoulder would ache but always the pain in my neck. I tried everything: physical therapy, massage therapy, hot and cold packs as well as hot and cold showers. I tried hot tubs and whirlpools along with an assortment of prescription medicine, but every relief was temporary.

I finally had to admit: the pain was not temporary. I had to learn to live with discomfort and some activities, once taken for granted, had to be curtailed. I had not appreciated my painless years. Perhaps they will return, but for now, I have to accept my discomfort and my pain as a price to pay for life.

Remember, life is temporary we have no guarantees . . . we have no assurances that we will survive to live our dreams and reach our goals. We must start living in the now. We must start celebrating the anquish and pain as the price we pay for life.

Some years ago, when I was surviving a series of traumatic and unhappy events in my life, a good friend had sent me a copy of a poem. I taped the poem on the mirror over my bathroom lavatory and I read it every day. I internalized its message. The poem made a difference in my life as I learned to stop whining about my problems. I learned to stop reliving and regretting the past and I examined what I truly believed. I conceived a vision of the way I wanted my life to be through looking at reality and envisioning dreams one day at a time. I began to control my life and accomplish goals I had felt were only dreams. I began to celebrate every day, every relationship, every event . . . one day at a time.

The poem's message reminded me to keep experiences in perspective. I needed the words then and I especially needed the message renewed after the car accident. This poem continues to be a source of comfort as life presents its daily challenges.

The author is unknown to me, but if, by chance a reader knows the reference, I will be happy to give credit in the future.

Celebrate The Temporary

Celebrate the temporary!
Don't wait until tomorrow—live today!
Celebrate the simple things. Enjoy a butterfly,
Embrace the snow, run with the ocean.
Delight in the trees or a single lonely flower.
Go barefoot in the wet grass!

Don't wait until all your problems are solved
Or all the bills are paid. You will wait forever.
Eternity will come and go and you will still be waiting.
Live in the now with all its problems and its agonies,
With its joy and pain.
Celebrate your pain, your despair, your anger.
It means you are alive.
Look closer, breathe deeper, stand taller.
Stop grieving the past!
There is joy and beauty in today.
But it is temporary—here, now and gone—
So celebrate it while you can.
Celebrate the temporary!

Life is a series of temporary celebrations. Through this book, I hope that you will enjoy and cherish your own temporary celebrations, remembering that the best that life offers is in the present—the here and now.

May God bless you as you continue to celebrate life.

J.J.R.

Celebrate the Temporary

"Don't be a
    stick-in-the-mud
Don't be a fool
You gotta understand—
There is life
    after school."

STORIES

of Family and Friends

And the Bride Wore Red

When our twenty-six year old daughter, Keri, called and said she had met the man of her dreams, my husband and I were impressed! She had gone through college without so much as even a discussion of any future plans that involved a permanent relationship with the opposite sex. She was committed to a career as an actress. That was all she had ever wanted to be. Her talent was obvious and the pursuit of her dream consumed her every minute. There was little time for boys and as she matured—for men. Now she was suddenly announcing that she had found Mr. Right. She wanted to bring him home to meet us.

"Don't tell Daddy," she warned. "I want it to be a surprise."

This Mr. Right, Raymond, was evidently raised with pure Southern charm and grace, she explained. He wanted to appear on our doorstep and ask her Daddy for his daughter's hand in the true old-South tradition.

I kept my promise, as hard as it was. Not knowing when this starry-eyed couple might appear, I spent much of the day looking out the front windows. My husband had many reasons not to be home on the appointed day but I insisted he keep busy with a list of household chores—the last of which was to fix the porch light. In mid-afternoon, when they drove up, my husband was teetering from a ladder holding dangling wire. None too soon, this newly-anointed knight in shining armor helped dismount his future father-in-law while introductions were made.

As rehearsed, our daughter told me that we needed to go shopping. Off we went to find something to occupy our time while the deed was done. After riding around for an hour observing town changes since her last visit, I quizzed her. "Don't you think we better go home?"

"Absolutely not," she responded. "They are probably just getting started and we would spoil it."

Rain came and we visited friends, drank coffee, and finally returned home after two hours. As we entered the house, we could hear the ball game blaring from the den television. The two of them sat calmly watching a game, saying nothing.

Our daughter was nervous. What if nothing had happened? She sat on the arm of her daddy's chair and asked, "Well, how did it go?"

Her daddy said, "This young man has just asked me for your hand and I told him 'I thought no one would ever ask' and that was it. Where have you been?"

The deed was done. Everyone relaxed. During their weekend stay, we were hosts to a wedding dinner for the son of friends of ours. Keri and Raymond helped with every detail. "After all, we've both worked at restaurants," they explained.

We talked in sketches about the wedding ceremony, set the date, changed the date, and narrowed down the places. "A garden wedding—small with all our friends. That's what I want," Keri explained.

Definitely different, the wedding would be unlike any we'd attended or read about. Held in an outdoor garden of a beautiful restaurant on a lake in a nearby town, it would be a day with old friends and forgotten faces.

Temporary lists were made; initial inquiries concerning prices and a budget of sorts defined. On Sunday, after they left for Dallas, my husband and I were convinced Raymond was the right man for Keri. They were very much in love.

In the next few months, preparations were set with long

distance decisions. Keri was organized and decisive. "Don't worry about the ceremony. We'll write our own vows."

While we visited her one weekend, our daughter secretly announced to us that her dress would not be the traditional white gown. "I look so pale in white," she explained. "I want something bright. I've found a beautiful red dress."

Although a little shocked, we all agreed it was her decision. In fact, for Keri, it seemed appropriate. She was not traditional; she was unique. We were pleased.

In the car on the way back home, my husband asked, "What will Mama Buck say?"

Mama Buck was his mother—a staunch traditional Southerner. I reminded my husband of a story about a lady who married late in life and was so happy that she ordered her house painted red inside and outside. We decided that red was the perfect color for our bride. After all, Mama Buck wanted Keri to be happy. She'd understand.

Shortly before the wedding date, Mama Buck had surgery and it would be impossible for her to attend the wedding. She would be recovering in the hospital. She was sorely disappointed and Keri knew it.

"We'll have a video, Mama Buck," Keri promised. But she could tell that wouldn't be the same.

The day before the wedding, Keri and Raymond appeared at the hospital in their full wedding attire. Mama Buck was in for a special treat. She would hear their original vows first, before anyone else, in the privacy of her hospital room. If she was shocked about the red dress, we never knew it.

Like her dress, Keri had definite ideas about the ceremony. She insisted, "Daddy, I don't want you to say that you are giving me away. I just want you to say something—whatever you want."

The morning of the wedding we arrived early at the wedding scene. The gates were closed and we were forced to sit in our car to wait for the owners to arrive. It allowed us a needed chance to catch our breath. I asked my husband, "Do you know what you will say today?"

"Not really. I haven't had much time to think about it," he answered. "What do you think about this?"

He practiced a few times and each time his words were different. We decided whatever he said it would be better for it to be unrehearsed.

The gates were opened; a dear friend appeared and the three of us hurriedly rearranged plants and flowers working with the restaurant crew to make the scene perfect. The day was beautiful; the weather was clear and the lake was sparkling. As we gathered debris from the grounds, we commented how lucky we were that the storms of the previous week were over.

Our friend asked about rice bags. We had forgotten. "No, bird seed would be better," we agreed. My husband raced to the store and returned with netting, ribbon, and seed. Our sons sat down and, after a quick lesson, produced the bags in record time.

The bride and her sister arrived and dressed in the upstairs dining room. Family mixed and mingled, arriving early.

Every detail showed her uniqueness. A tiered white wedding cake, but instead of the traditional bride and groom at the top stood figures of cartoon characters He-Man and She-Rah, a private joke between the couple. A local disc jockey, dressed in formal tux and tails, spun pre-recorded classical music chosen by the bride and groom. In the midst of the arrival of guests, Keri and Raymond casually appeared and visited with friends and relatives an hour before the ceremony. There were no posed wedding photographs; candid shots were plentiful.

Promptly at noon, the music stopped, to begin again with the Hallelujah chorus at the conclusion of the ceremony. Keri's aunts and cousins, stationed throughout the garden, began to shake assorted small bells. It was a sign for the parents to make their way through the guests to chairs placed in the corner of the garden. The preacher, a cousin of the bride, walked to his

appointed stance. The bridegroom and his father took their places.

It was a day to remember—a beautiful brunch, dancing and laughter, but what will be indelibly etched upon our minds is what her father said as he escorted his daughter to Raymond's hand.

He turned to the young man and spoke distinctly and clearly, "We come here today to celebrate life and celebrate love. We bring Keri to you, Raymond, and we hope you will love and cherish her as much as we do."

She was our beautiful bride in red.

Surprise Celebration

My husband turned 50 a few years ago and I was determined that he would be treated to a much-needed vacation as my gift to him. He loved to scuba dive, but had little time to enjoy the sport. He would sit and look at travel agency brochures and dream of exploring faraway reefs.

My sister lived in another state and we had wanted to take a trip together, but it was hard to coordinate our calendars. She called and discussed her plans for a trip to Mexico. "The diving is wonderful," she tempted. "They say Cozumel is a diver's paradise. Why don't you two join us there?"

Business appointments kept us from making long range plans and the trip she offered, though a bargain, would require advance booking. That was impossible—or was it?

For weeks before his birthday, I carefully and secretly planned and organized his celebration. With the help of his secretary, we cleared his calendar for two and a half days. Coupled with a weekend and Monday holiday and with the help of a patient travel agent, he would have his needed vacation.

The travel package included air fare from a nearby city and motel costs. But how was I going to get him out of the office? He would resist. My husband is a dentist. He loves to work and he hates surprises.

On his birthday, the secretary had arranged the appointment book to look even busier than usual. He thought he had a long list of patients. It would be a hectic day, or so he thought.

"I'll have him arrested," I told my sister. "We have a friend who is a policeman. He can arrest him for turning 50 and sentence him to a long weekend of fun. We'll have some of our friends there, a birthday cake, and they will help me get him out the door."

I talked to the officer friend and he agreed to be a part of the conspiracy if we could wait until he was off duty. We agreed.

The day before we were to leave I packed our clothes and put the suitcases in the trunk of the car. I told our children and called a few friends to meet us at the office for a surprise birthday party. We were set.

The next day, I went to the office and sat in the waiting room. The friends arrived, but no policeman. Our daughter drove in from out of town with her video camera. Our son was there. My husband kept right on working as we quietly anticipated the fun. So as not to frighten the patient who would be there when he was "arrested", the secretary revealed the plan to this final patient. The patient laughed and thought it was a great gag. We were ready to do the evil deed.

But the policeman was late and my husband ran ahead of schedule. He finished with the patient and began to work on a walk-in, someone who had no appointment and knew nothing of our trick.

The policeman entered the back door, went to the operatory, and told the shocked and embarrassed dentist that he had a warrant for his arrest. Not wanting the patient to think badly of him, the officer was asked to wait in the back office.

"No, sir. We need to take care of this right here," the officer said. Thinking the patient knew the trick, he produced a set of handcuffs and began to read the charges:

> You are hereby charged with unlawfully and unknowingly, without due consideration for your peers, colleagues, or patients and with no forethought and with unconscionable disregard for tomorrow, with

approaching the half-century mile marker at speeds above and beyond reasonable limits.

And the sentence: "Being found without due representation and guilty of the above charges, you are hereby sentenced to six days of hard rest and relaxation."

The patient jumped out of the chair after the "You are hereby charged with . . . .", and, still wearing his bib, ran out of the office.

In total shock, my husband donned a shirt which read, "Feeling Nifty; Turning Fifty," and blew out the candles on his birthday cake. He opened his gifts, thanked everyone, and nervously attempted to end the party. He wanted the fun to be over; he needed to see his patients. As the staff continued to enjoy the revelry, he walked to the waiting room. It was empty. Horns were blowing as cars passed by. He glanced out the window and saw the sign across the building: "Dr. Roebuck is 50 today."

He returned to the party and asked his secretary where the patients were. There were none.

"We might as well go home," I suggested. "You have nothing to do today."

Skeptical but encouraged by his staff and friends, he headed for the car.

"I'll drive," I offered. Leaving the parking lot, I didn't make the usual turn toward home, but traveled out of town.

"Where are you going?" he asked.

When I didn't reply, he said, "Oh, I'll bet I know. We're having dinner out of town. How sweet!"

As we traveled, he slept. When he awoke we were almost to the airport exit.

"Are we going on a trip? I have no clothes," he said.

And then, "Mexicana Airlines! Where the thunder are we going?" he yelled as I opened the trunk to reveal suitcases.

We boarded a plane for Cozumel and he was still in shock. He asked questions, "How long will we be gone? . . . What about my appointments tomorrow? . . . How did you arrange all this without me knowing?"

All I would answer is, "It's all taken care of."

We landed and were taken to our hotel. While we stood at the desk checking in, I spotted my sister and her husband sitting in the lobby, the final surprise of the day.

Receiving our room assignment, we started for the elevator and my sister met us at the stairs.

"Excuse me, sir," she said as she accidentally bumped into my husband.

He looked up to see her and her husband standing there.

"Happy birthday, brother-in-law," she said as she kissed him on the cheek.

My husband smiled and said, "I'll tell you one thing. To start out like any other, this has been the most exciting day I've ever had. I'm beginning to like surprises. What's next?"

Parents Grow Up, Too!

After my parents sold our farm, they moved to the town where my sister and I lived. They enjoyed weekend trips with friends and relatives. They had spent their lifetime saving for a little comfort. They loved to travel. One particular Friday, they told my sister and me they were going for a few days of fun on the Gulf Coast with my aunt and uncle, retired schoolteachers from another state. The trip to the Coast would take three hours. We assumed they would be back on Sunday. Late Sunday afternoon, we straightened their house, readying it for my aunt and uncle to spend the night before leaving for their home the next day. We turned on lamps and outside lights to welcome them.

Late that evening, my sister called and said she had checked their house and they had not returned. I assured her that they must have spent the night along the way.

"Don't worry," I comforted her. "They are always fine."

As soon as I hung up, I called the motel where they always stayed, but the desk clerk said they had checked out. I was worried and I'm sure my sister was concerned, but we assured each other that this was nothing.

By noon on Monday, when they did not answer their phone, from our work phones my sister and I called the highway department to see if there were known problems.

The dispatcher appeared annoyed, "Weather is clear and we have no problems on the highway from here to the Coast. No reported accidents."

Still concerned, during lunch we divided the towns along the route and called hospitals checking to see if any of them were patients. We found no clues.

By late afternoon, we were beside ourselves with worry. We were both waiting at their house when they came pulling into the driveway, laughing and talking. We were mad and glad at the same time.

"What are you all doing here?" our daddy quizzed.

When we explained our worry, none of them could believe our concern. We couldn't believe it. We had spent our entire weekend worrying about our parents.

Daddy took us aside and said, "You are grown girls now. You have your own families and your own homes. You have enough to do without worrying about us. Your mother and I have waited all our lives for the chance to do what we want. Now we are doing it. When we leave on a trip, don't worry about us. We may be back when we say or we might stay longer or come home earlier. Just remember, we're grown, too."

Today, my mother is 75 and my father is 81. They travel around the country in their pick-up truck pulling a travel trailer. While some people spend many hours organizing itineraries with detailed plans, our parents often do not know where they are going, when they will get there, or when they will return. Sometimes we know when they leave and we might have a general idea of when they will return. But one thing for sure, we have never let them know if we are worried.

Get with the program
Use some zap and zest
You only go around
*   once*
Life is NOT
a multiple choice test.

I Didn't Know
I Was An Environmentalist

"Hazardous Waste Disposal Site" was what the newspaper called it. I heard some friends refer to it as a recycling plant and others as a temporary incinerator.

I had no opinion at the meeting. Both sides left unanswered questions but I didn't want to get involved. I had too much on my mind and too many other projects.

As I was leaving the meeting, a friend touched me on the back and whispered, "I didn't know you were an environmentalist."

What a supreme compliment he had paid me. If attending a meeting to gather information about a possible hazardous waste disposal site classifies one as an environmentalist then I suppose I was and am. But further thought and study revealed that all of us should be environmentalists.

We should all be concerned about the air, the water, and our environment. How inadequately we display an appreciation for these God-given gifts! Our generation has taken the atmosphere for granted. We have done little to preserve it and everything to destroy it. We pollute, we abuse, and we under-replenish what we use. We have no appreciation for what our fathers and grandfathers worked to protect and maintain. We clear-cut and over-develop.

We think of today with expediency rather than tomorrow and the consequences of our deeds. We read about toxic waste and the effects of polychlorinated biphenyls (PCB's). We destroy the ozone layer, but we continue to use Styrofoam cups, enjoy aerosol cans, and fertilize our yards. We cut our hardwoods and replace them with pines; we mow our yards and burn the clippings. We throw our bottles and cans in the land fills and call the recyclists strange and a little nutty. We run too much water and throw out tons of garbage. We cut down trees to make our grass grow greener or strip the branches for better reception from our television satellite dishes. We draw house plans and clear the trees to fit the plan rather than the opposite. Backhoe operators nick and scrape the trees and rationalize, "They're strong; they'll recover." Expediency is the rule.

We think our Earth will last forever, but in reality we know it can't. We tell our grandchildren of the wonder of the universe as we destroy it bit by bit.

I was no different from the rest. I had welcomed paper plates and Styrofoam cups. Our family cleared the woods to increase our farm land. We had no regard for the animals that made their home in the trees. Today, the wooded pasture is cleared. I remembered my childhood of fun in those woods. I visualized a hot summer day, the temperature rising, and our cows huddled together under a remaining clump of cool oaks.

My mind raced as I silently chastised myself for not being more actively involved in protecting our environment. A friend was sitting beside me and as we waited for more testimony, she talked of her personal battle to turn weeds into wildflowers.

She explained, "Life deals us many small pleasures and perhaps even a few large ones. One of the smallest may be the opportunity to enjoy the wildflowers along our nation's highways. But even small pleasures may soon be vanishing."

She had the ear of a few around her. "We're poisoning the right-of-ways and the medians on our interstates as well as state and county roads. We've turned the pretty clumps of black-eyed Susans and wild yarrow into tall skinny stalks of bloomless weeds. Why?"

She answered her own question, "Because it makes it easier to cut and mow, and we cut and mow because it enables us to easily identify and retrieve litter along our byways. Think about it—if we didn't poison and we didn't mow, perhaps the mountains of litter wouldn't be so noticeable. Those adopting stretches of highways could still find the paper and cans."

She was on her soapbox and she had an audience. "We could look to the left and the right and see the vast differences of color splattered along the road in the form of beautiful and distinctly different wildflowers."

She was a teacher and we were her students. "In our state, over six hundred varieties of wildflowers have been identified, and in other states, even more. But we're killing them with poison. Many won't reseed. Some species we'll never see again.

"It's ironical. We pass laws outlawing litter and we threaten to prosecute those who do. Yet our highways are dirty and in our state alone we spend over $700,000 every year to collect litter and many thousands more to mow and poison. If we spent only a portion of that on cultivating wildflowers, we'd be better off."

As she talked, I thought of my tenth-grade son who had a biology project on wildflowers. He had a choice of actually gathering and mounting a collection of fifty species of wildflowers, organizing a photography album, or video. He chose the photography project. As usual, he put the work off until the last few weeks of the school year.

By the time he loaded his camera for his day in the flowers, the highway and road departments had done their spring cleaning. They poisoned and mowed the byways and the beautiful wildflowers were all but gone. Luckily, we were making a trip to a neighboring state where the philosophy is different. They do not mow their roadsides and medians, but leave them natural with hundreds of varieties of wildflowers. So the project was saved by our sister state. Today we revel in the beauty of the photographs.

As I recollected the experience, the friend joked, "Yes, things are always greener on the other side of the fence."

Her attitude changed to serious. She admonished us. "We must learn to accept inconvenience as the price to pay for a safe, beautiful, and clean atmosphere."

We knew she was right. The battle could be won by small groups and individuals like those gathered at our courthouse that night. We left, more firmly committed to teach our students and our children new ways to live safely and securely while maintaining an aesthetic world for those who follow.

So, yes, friend, I am an environmentalist. I just hope I can live up to the title.

Old Shep

It was Christmas and as we always did, we were staying at Ma-Maw's. Everyone was there, all the aunts and uncles and all my cousins. We were all over the house. The children had carefully written their letters to Santa advising him that he must bring presents to us at her house.

This particular Christmas was different. Ma-Maw had a little dog that she dearly loved. She even loved him enough to let him come inside . . . not in the main part of the house, mind you, but she did let him come on the porch. I knew she loved him because even though she'd be upset about something, her tone of voice would change when she talked to the dog.

On Christmas Eve, there was a lot of coming and going with all the people staying at Ma-Maw's. The next morning, bright and early, I awoke to hear people whispering and talking about Ma-Maw's dog. "Somebody ran over Charley. He's dead," Mother explained to my sister and me. "The men are burying him out behind the garage."

They said when Ma-Maw found him in the driveway, she didn't cry. I'm not surprised because I don't ever remember seeing her cry. She asked about the coming and going the night before. No one would admit they had run over Charley.

After they finished burying him, I watched from the window, and Ma-Maw went back behind the garage and stayed a long time. When she came back in the kitchen to check on the dinner, her eyes were red and she was sniffing, but none of us grandkids said anything.

I was only eight, but I knew how it felt, or I thought I did. We had a dog at home and I loved him, too. I knew how I'd feel if Old Shep got run over and we had to bury him.

We left Ma-Maw's late that afternoon and we didn't talk much about Charley. Mother said she felt sorry for Ma-Maw because the dog had been such company for her. When we got home, my Daddy walked out and petted Old Shep and said, "You know, girls, I think it would be a real good idea if we gave Shep to Ma-Maw. I think he'd really like it there."

Well, I knew he wouldn't. He wouldn't like it at all because I wouldn't be there and after all, she lived an hour away and we didn't go there but every other Sunday and on Thanksgiving and Christmas.

I said, "No, Daddy, let's don't give Old Shep away. He wouldn't like it."

But Daddy insisted, "Yeah, we need to because your grandmother is out in the country by herself and she needs a dog and Old Shep will be good to her and she'll be good to Old Shep, too. She loved her dog and she'll love Old Shep just the same."

Every night my sister and I would talk about it and we would cry, but Daddy had his mind made up and we knew he wouldn't change it. Even my mother, who didn't care for any dog, tried to talk him out of it, but when my Daddy's mind was made up, no one could make him change it. He was determined Ma-Maw would have the dog. We could see him when we went to visit. The next Sunday we put Old Shep in the car and we took him to Ma-Maw's house.

When we drove up, Old Shep jumped out of the car, looked around, and jumped right back in on top of me. He'd checked it out and he didn't like it. "Did you see that, Daddy? I told you Old Shep wouldn't like it here."

I was determined that I wouldn't let Ma-Maw know how sad I was because then she wouldn't let Old Shep stay, and it was supposed to keep her from being so lonely. It would cheer her up, but when we told her that we brought her Old Shep, she got mad and said, "I don't know why you brought that dog. I don't want it. Can't any dog take Charley's place. I'm just fine. Take the dog home."

Daddy told us not to say anything; that we'd leave him and after we were gone, Old Shep would make friends with Ma-Maw and they'd both be fine.

That afternoon, my sister and I played with Old Shep outside and we told him that he had to stay. It didn't do much good, though, because when we left, he tried to chase the car and we had to finally go back and tie him up out by the garden. That made us real upset because Old Shep had never been tied up before. He looked so sad; he didn't understand. He'd always been free to run up and down the fields and pasture around our house.

I sat on my knees and stared out the back car window until I couldn't see Ma-Maw's house anymore. I moved my lips, "Bye, Old Shep. I'll see you soon." I cried a little and bit my lip. Daddy was looking in the rear view mirror, and I tried to be brave. So did my sister, and I know she was sad, too, but we didn't say anything.

Two weeks later, after church, we drove to Ma-Maw's to eat dinner like we always did. As soon as we drove up, Old Shep came running to us wagging his tail and trying to lick us. I kneeled down and he licked me all over my face. I knew he'd missed me. I went inside and I asked Ma-Maw how he was doing.

She said, "You know, he's a pretty good dog. He doesn't bark at my friends, but he barks at strangers. He doesn't chase cars."

I felt mighty proud when she said that. I was the one that had cured him of chasing cars. He used to be real bad, and on our gravel road the cars would speed along and he would run after them. One day a car hit him. It wasn't bad, but he had a lame leg to show for it. I had given him a pretty bad scolding and I could see in his eyes that he'd learned his lesson.

Ma-Maw kept talking about Old Shep, "At night, he doesn't want to come inside; he just crawls up under the house and finds a cool place that he's dug up under there. He seems to like it. I know you miss him."

"Yes, I do miss him," I admitted, "But you need a dog more than we do. We're in school anyway and Old Shep was lonely." I tried to think of all the reasons why he needed to live with her and not me, but I still didn't understand.

And so from then on, every other Sunday we'd go see Old Shep. I really felt bad because it got to where I looked forward more to seeing Old Shep than I did to seeing Ma-Maw, but I guess it was O.K. because my sister said she felt the same way.

About three years later my uncle called and said that Old Shep had died. He had buried him out behind the garage next to Charley. That Sunday when we got to Ma-Maw's, my sister and I took two old boards and nailed them together and carved "Old Shep" across the top. We put the cross out by his grave and we told him one final good-bye. Ma-Maw thanked us and we knew that she had grown to love him as much as we had.

Many years later, after my Daddy died, my uncle was telling us stories one night and he told the story of Ma-Maw's dog, Charley. He had gone into town with my daddy that Christmas Eve, and as they were backing out of the driveway, they had run over the dog. It was too long ago, he couldn't remember who was driving. If he did, he didn't tell.

I thought back and I knew then why Daddy had had to give up Old Shep. Probably, at that time, it made him feel better. He loved Old Shep just like we did, but since he had taken her dog, we had to give her ours.

Living in the Past—
I'll destroy my soul!

Living in the Future—
I'll lose control!

But living in the Present—
I'll be whole!

The Day Daddy
Kept His Temper

I grew up in the country—the real country. Not just a few miles but a long seven and one-half miles from the city limits of a small Mississippi Delta town. In the 40's and 50's it didn't seem fashionable to admit one lived in the country. In fact, those of us living on the New Africa Road in the Mississippi Delta were sometimes referred to as "country hicks."

In earlier days, playthings were created from existing sources. Paper dolls were cut from mail order catalogs; doll house furniture was crafted from candy boxes rescued from the burn pile behind the small commissary that my mother operated from our back yard.

As I grew older, none of my friends seemed to envy my country residence, and when I turned twelve my parents allowed me to accept a few invitations from friends to stay in town on a weekend. I wanted to invite them to the country, but what could I offer them? Feeding pigs and endless chores. Hayrides and tractor jaunts were fun and Daddy might allow both if he was in a good mood— which meant it hadn't rained too much and the sun had shone just right, and the cotton was coming up, neatly chopped, or already picked.

Perhaps other country friends could treat their guests to a horse, but all I had to offer was a Massey-Ferguson 300 tractor. It was my constant and faithful companion. The small tractor could be maneuvered easily for pleasure rides in the fields and on the country roads.

One spring Friday afternoon, my friend Cynthia came to spend the night with me. I promised her it would be fun. As soon as we got off the bus, we changed our clothes and boarded the tractor. Starting out from the shed, we traveled into the remote regions of our Delta farm, far into paths overgrown with underbrush. I was in complete control—showing my town friend just how wonderful it was to live in the country. She was hard to convince. She reminded me over and over that her mother didn't want her to get dirty and she was afraid of bugs. The slow grinding, never-ceasing sounds of the machine disturbed Nature at Her finest afternoon hour. We were obvious intruders weaving our way down untraveled paths. Cynthia, sitting on the hump of metal over the big tractor tire, bumped

along imagining aloud what our other friends must be doing in town.

We guided our way into the fields, laughing and talking. Without warning, quick chokes caused a jolt and sputter; the tractor was suddenly dumb. Smoke bellowed from the sides of the hood. Arrogantly, insisting I could fix the problem, I climbed down from my driver's perch and proudly lifted the hood as I had seen my father do many times. Burning my fingers attempting to release the latch, I hid the pain and anger. I couldn't see anything wrong. Cynthia didn't seem impressed. She said she wanted to go home. After many attempts at cranking, we were both disgusted and weary.

With her new pair of shorts and sandals, my indication that we had to walk home seemed to make her angry. I promised her that if we hurried, we could be there before dark. We started out across a path that had not been traveled since the cotton pickers left the previous season. Tangled webs of vines and weeds made an insect-infested jungle and we were soon frustrated and tired. We tried to find another route but none were better. We said nothing. I looked at Cynthia's legs and they were bleeding from the sticker vines pushing against us as we walked. I offered her my socks, but she just shook her head and pouted.

All I could think of was how wonderful it must be in town and I knew she was thinking the same. If only I had gone home with Cynthia for the weekend! We could be at Garmon's Ice Cream Parlor or shopping at Powers Department Store, but no, I had to show her how wonderful it was to drive a tractor. I had to be a smart-aleck and independent showout! I didn't even check with Daddy before I took the tractor.

It was getting dark and the hush was frightening . . . that long-lasting Delta quiet with noises like no other place—trees swaying and rustling in the premature spring breeze; small rabbits stirring the brush and, although I said nothing, I could imagine snakes slithering underneath the moist grass. Locusts were humming loudly, competing with a bee buzzing around our heads.

I admonished Cynthia, "Don't swat at him; he won't sting you."

Birds continued to chirp an evening song accompanied by water dripping down the furrows into ditches below. There was a sweet smell which meant that rain had come only hours before. Normally, this scene would have made me glad to be in the country. Today, I was embarrassed to admit it was my home.

What had I done? I wondered in silence. What will Daddy do to me?

I knew I would be punished and Cynthia would be taken home. I would be forbidden to drive the tractor again. Tears welled in my eyes and a lump lodged in my throat. I stared straight ahead and pushed back the briars with a stick I'd found.

Finally, I could see the back of our old barn and Daddy cranking the Farmall tractor to come and look for us. I yelled; Cynthia screamed. He walked toward us. Like most Delta farmers, my daddy was not known for his patience, and his temperament was often gruff. I prayed he wouldn't fuss at me in front of Cynthia, but I knew he would. I ran toward him so any scolding might escape Cynthia's ears.

"Where's the tractor?" he yelled when I was closer.

"It wouldn't start," I explained, "but it will be O.K. I left it in the lower field by the woods."

Daddy's eyes darted at Cynthia, back at me, but he said nothing. Cynthia walked past us and didn't stop until she had found the water faucet by the chickenhouse and she washed her legs under the cool water.

When she was out of hearing range, I whispered to Daddy, "I didn't do anything to make it quit; I was just driving it slow—real slow through the fields."

He looked angry, glanced toward Cynthia, and said nothing more than, "Go to the house with your friend. It's too late to see about it today. We'll go first thing in the morning."

Mother offered to take Cynthia home, but I pleaded with her to stay. She was my weekend reprieve and I didn't want her to leave and think badly of me. We bathed and put on clean clothes while Mother fixed supper. Cynthia wanted to watch television, but I wanted to stay out of Daddy's way so we avoided the den at the back of the house.

Supper was eaten with only polite conversation. After helping with the dishes, Cynthia and I caught lightning bugs in a mayonnaise jar and took them with us to the little house in the back yard. It was an old smoke house which had been roughly converted for an extra bedroom. It was just large enough for an old iron bed. We stayed up late playing Monopoly. I was nice . . . I let Cynthia win. We tuned in a radio music show and sang along to the familiar tunes of rock and roll.

Early in the morning, Daddy called to me from outside the screened window. I jumped up dressing, trying hard not to awaken Cynthia. She slept. I met Daddy at the shed, riding silently with him to the field where the abandoned tractor sat. I was scared of what we'd find. What had I done? When I was ten, Daddy had patiently taught me to drive the tractor and allowed me the privilege of driving in the fields around the house. The unwritten rule was that I check with him before I drove it. I had violated that trust. I would be punished and I would lose the privilege of the tractor.

Daddy raised the hood and checked the radiator. "Umph! Just like I thought. Didn't you check the tractor before you tried to show out for your friend?"

"No, sir," I answered. "Is there something wrong?"

"Sure is!" he yelled. "Really wrong! You've seen to it that the tractor is burned up."

With that he cranked up the Farmall and I raced to grab onto the back of his seat, riding on the raised plow back to the barn. He drove the tractor into the open side of the shed and said, "You go on and tend to your company. I'll get one of the hands to go with me to tow her in."

He wasn't mad; he didn't yell. I ran back to the little house and awoke Cynthia. We rode bikes, played with the cats in the barn, and swung on the vines in the woods pretending to be friends of Tarzan. Daddy never mentioned the tractor.

That afternoon, when it was time to take Cynthia back into town she didn't want to go. It was her first visit to the country and just as she had begun to like it, it was over. I didn't want her to go. I knew my time for punishment was coming. She was my protector. Without her, Daddy would begin his scolding.

After she entered her house and we drove away, I waited for his words, but they never came. We carried out our usual Saturday ritual. We drove downtown, around the Main Street block until we found a place in the area where we always parked—in front of Woolworth's. Daddy got out of the car, standing leaning on the parking meter smoking cigarettes and talking with other farmers.

"It's lightning in the southwest. There'll be rain by morning," Daddy forecasted.

My sister was older and she was allowed to meet a friend and go to the picture show across the street. When Mother and I were alone, I asked if Daddy had decided what my punishment would be. She said, "He's not talked about the tractor."

Mother and I went into stores and walked down the street. We looked and window shopped. I spent my 50-cent allowance. Mother bought a 10-cent bag of popcorn and we sat in the car eating and watching people pass. Occasionally, a friend would walk by, wave, and some would stop to talk, but mainly I worried.

Mother told me that if I was really down in the dumps to start watching people and try to imagine their problems. She and I talked about the folks who walked down the street: big people, little people, old people, young people. Occasionally there would be someone handicapped and my mother would remind me of how fortunate I was to be normal and healthy. I really concentrated on faces. Were they worried like me?

The stores closed at 9:00 and shortly afterward the picture show ended. We drove by the bakery and bought a box of freshly baked bread. There were five loaves in the box. As usual, on the way home we opened a loaf. It was warm and the aroma filled the car. We ate the slices. I kept waiting for the punishment and admonishment, but it never came. All day Sunday, Daddy never talked about the tractor. In fact, he never mentioned it again.

Monday morning, by the time our bus arrived at school, Cynthia had told all the girls what a fun time she'd had and how exciting it was to live on a farm. At last, I felt I had something to offer the city girls: the country with its bees, wet fields, pigs, locusts, and my Massey-Ferguson 300 tractor. It was my world and now my town friends wanted to be a part of it too.

Lessons from Mother

Mother taught me important things. Lessons that are hard to forget. Some of them I will teach to my children and some I will not.

Mother said to drink eight glasses of water every day—not cold, not hot— room temperature. She drank a glass as soon as she got up and a glass before she went to bed. She mixed six in between. She has been healthy, has flawless skin and few wrinkles, and today she's 75. I should find this habit easy to adopt, but I don't.

She required that we drink a quart of milk a day—not pasteurized or homogenized, but cow's virgin milk, straight from our farm. She insisted that we would be healthier and our bodies stronger. My sisters and I fought this requirement, and with our spoon or knife would skim the cream off the top of the milk, closing our eyes as we drank for fear we would see the cream we had missed. We would encourage company to drink our quota, a reprieve Mother allowed.

Mother insisted that our rooms be kept clean, our drawers neat, and that we sort through our things and give away clothes and trinkets on a regular basis to the children of the farm workers. She would morbidly but jokingly say, "Clean up your room before we leave the house. We may be brought back in feet first and then our friends and the neighbors will see it as we leave it."

Today, as we leave for work or a trip, I find myself scurrying around picking up and organizing, remembering those words. Mother taught a lot of lessons by example. Lists were important to her. Little scraps of paper, writings in spiral notebooks, endless notes—reminders of duties completed and those yet to do. Today, my first daily duty is my "To Do" list and I feel great satisfaction in marking off the accomplishments one by one at the end of the day.

Mother was the ninth of ten children and raised on a 700-acre farm in Leflore County in the Mississippi Delta. Like me, she learned lessons from her mother well. She could stretch a dollar as far as she needed, to take care of her family. She managed the books for my father's farm as her mother, our Ma-Maw, had done after the death of my grandfather. She could always produce the funds to buy our necessities—though we had only what was absolutely required.

Like me also, Mother gives her mother credit for her organization and tenacity. She says, "I inherited being boss, taking over things and knowing what I had to do."

She learned many lessons in financial survival. She taught those lessons to my two sisters and me. For years, she played housewife to my farmer father. She raised three daughters and helped support the family by selling fresh milk, butter, and eggs door to door. My sisters and I would play in the back seat of the car as she drove into the back driveways of the largest and prettiest houses in town to place her goods in the customer's refrigerators, even if they were away from home.

My sisters and I accompanied her to homes around our farm to conduct the 1950 census. She carefully asked the questions required on the detailed form and recorded information about the farm families and their possessions. One day she realized she had missed a question and we were loaded into the car to return to the Grattafori farm to complete the form. Mr. Grattafori, seeing our car entering his driveway, came out of his house and yelled, "My God, woman, what you want now?

You want to see if my hen laid an egg last night?"

At the Crocker farmhouse, Mother asked her census questions with sincerity.

"What is your religion?"

Young Mr. Crocker answered with a serious tone, "Camel light."

As he watched Mother write "Campbellite" on the form, he laughingly explained, "The Camel died and the light went out."

Patiently, without displaying her obvious frustration, Mother took out another form to begin again as Mr. Crocker howled with laughter.

Mother was meticulous with her money and required that we follow her example. She insisted that we keep a list of what we spent and she examined the record regularly.

She never gave money to us without its being earned. We had to work at various chores. We stood our duty at the commissary, which was a "store" converted from an unused cotton storage house retrieved from the cotton fields on our farm. Set on concrete blocks, the small, one-room house was thirty feet from our back door. Windows were installed on two sides and a counter built across the middle with an open end for passage. Plank shelves filled with staples lined the back wall and a five-gallon jug holding pickled pig's feet sat on one counter end.

From this small room, we sold chewing tobacco, snuff, cigarettes, candy bars, moon pies, canned goods, crackers, and bread. Since there was no room for a refrigerator, the soft drinks, luncheon meats, and cheeses had to be dispensed from the farmhouse kitchen refrigerator and given to the farmhands through the screened porch back door. If we worked all day, our reward might be a Pepsi-Cola and a moon pie.

Housework was the regular Saturday agenda. The motivation for early rising and hard work was the promise of a trip to town in late afternoon to visit the stores which stayed open until nine o'clock on Saturday night. Dusting was almost endless since our farmhouse was on a gravel road and even the high, thick privet hedges could not keep out the billows of dust as cars traveled past. The soft pinewood floors required weekly waxings. After the wax was dry, pieces of an old red wool blanket, placed under our bare feet, buffed the wood to a glorious shine as we moved our bodies back and forth. If Mother and Daddy were gone, we might turn on the radio and twist to the popular songs of the fifties.

Yardwork was painful as we pruned and weeded flower beds of verbena and dusty miller, clipped hedges, and mowed the bermuda grass and weeds all the way to the electric barbed-wire fence which surrounded the pasture and woods. Bees and wasps loved the blooming crape myrtle bushes in the front yard, and pushing the mower under the limbs of the huge bushes would send the insects swarming at us. We lived with the discomfort of the stings and subsequent swelling as we did with mosquito bites and the resulting scars from endless scratching.

We sold watermelons and peanuts from our yard, the products of days of turning vines and digging in the dirt. In the fields on hot summer days, my sisters and I would form an assembly line loading the produce on the back of our old truck. Often we would 'accidentally' drop a melon.

"I'm sorry, Daddy, I didn't mean to," I would yell. "But we don't want it to go to waste. Can we eat it now?"

Daddy would try to look stern, and, pretending he didn't know it wasn't an accident, he would agree to the break.

"Save the seeds," he'd shout.

Digging into it with our bare hands, eating the ripe sweet meat, we would let the sticky juice drip down our faces. We would spit the seeds in one corner of the truck bed, carefully scooping them up at the end of the day. The seeds would be spread on newspaper on the back porch and, when completely dry, placed in jars. From this collection, Daddy would plant and create unique varieties.

Taking turns, we sat on the roadside hoping that a passerby would stop and buy the twenty-five cent melons, the dime cantaloupes, or nickel bags of peanuts. If the crop was especially prolific, the produce would be peddled in town from the parking lot of the Kroger store on Fourth Street. As my sisters and I grew older, we would dread hawking our goods at the grocery store. We lived in fear that some of our town friends would see us standing in the back of our pickup truck. It would be the only time we would argue over who would remain at home to work with Mother in the garden.

Our garden was situated behind the garage beside our house. Daddy would plow the ground and our mother would plant the vegetables and scold us into long days of chopping and weeding. Chicken and king snakes were prevalent and we worked with a watchful eye on the tall grass surrounding the crop. We sold the vegetables along with our milk and butter, after keeping enough for our own use.

Tending the farm animals was a daily and endless chore. My sisters milked our two cows and I was given the job of slopping the hogs, which consisted of carrying the bucket of food scraps, dishwater, and soured milk to the feeding trough in the muddy and smelly lot or barnyard. The hogs and piglets would run at me and 'oink' their pleasure.

The chickens had to be fed twice a day and eggs gathered in the late afternoon. The tin henhouse at the edge of the field had to be cleaned on a regular basis. The chicken manure was shoveled and used for garden fertilizer. The eggs were gathered from the straw nests inside the dark unlighted chicken house. From time to time, the person gathering the eggs would scream and run after feeling a snake in the nest.

For several years, my mother raised chicken fryers in the old pump house beside the tractor shed. She would order a hundred chicks from a mail-order catalog and place them in the two-tiered incubator or brooder in the dark confines of the house. The walls were foot-thick wood with a heavy door and dirt floor. The trays under each brooder had to be lined with newspaper and changed daily. It was a chore we dreaded. Often, chicks would be sick and my mother would nurse them on our back porch, feeding them Karo syrup from a medicine dropper and greasing their heads with lard until they were well and could return to their brooder. In six to eight weeks, as the chicks grew into fryers, we would spend our Saturdays processing them for freezing.

Daddy would take the fryer, holding the neck and wringing it until the body of the chicken went sailing into the yard, flopping its wings and spewing blood over the grass. My sister and I would run and catch the chicken by its feet and take it to my mother who would dip the fowl into a pot of boiling water brought from the kitchen. This loosened the feathers which were then plucked and the chicken's body singed clean by holding it over the flame of a fire built on the rubbish or burn pile by the pasture.

Mother would split open the body and clean out the entrails, saving the liver and gizzard. The chicken was then ready to be cut into pieces and packed into bags for the food freezer.

Because the farm pump water left yellow rust stains on whatever it touched, Mother would take the laundry to town and leave it to be washed and left damp. When she returned, we hung the clothes on the line strung between the garage and the peach tree.

In winter, we would don wool gloves for this chore, propping the wire as high as it would go with the handy notched wooden pole and retrieving the clothes often frozen stiff with ice. Clothes were placed everywhere inside—over doors and furniture—to dry.

Mother believed in regular saving, and our one and only family vacation trip was possible because, at her urging, everyone in the family saved a dime every day. Eagerly, my sisters and I put our shiny coins in tubular silver dime banks all year. When

they were full, Mother would count them one by one and add
our money to the family pool. We'd begin again. We were saving
for a trip to the Smoky Mountains of Tennessee. To us, it
seemed a fantasy.

But finally the trip happened! We had never been further
north than Memphis or in another state except Tennessee unless
you counted the Sunday ferry ride across the Mississippi River
into Arkansas. We took my parents' best friends along—six
of us in the old Chevrolet.

Although my oldest sister, Marjorie Ann, had carefully
saved her dimes and planned for the trip too, she was not able
to go. Several weeks before our departure, she landed her first
job. She would work during that summer as a secretary for
an attorney in town. Marjorie Ann gladly gave up the trip
because she was promised the lucrative salary of twenty

dollars a week. Mother arranged for her to stay with her friend Bertha Griffin. We were ready!

In the car, my other sister and I were kept busy inventing make-believe games of pretend as we alternated the middle seats in the front and back. We said little, listening to our parents and their friends Daisy and Paul Geleston marvel at the sights.

Daisy and Paul were farmers like our parents, but with no children of their own they had become "adopted" relatives to my sisters and me. Mrs. Geleston, as we were always required to call her, was a true Southern lady, using cloth napkins and her best silver when we would visit for a special meal.

As a child, I bit my fingernails unmercifully—a habit I was trying desperately to overcome. Mrs. Geleston chided me to quit and one Christmas gave me a nice manicure set packaged in a cardboard kit complete with polish, cuticle remover, nail

file, and buffer. It was so pretty and I promised her I would let my nails grow, but I didn't and each time we made our weekly visit to her nearby house, she would inspect my hands and silently shame me again and again. I wanted to cry each time I presented my hands and fingers to her to watch her slowly shake her head disapprovingly from side to side, saying nothing . . . but everything.

On the Smoky Mountain trip, I desperately tried to keep fingernail biting to a minimum. Each time I would put my hand to my mouth, I would feel her piercing eyes staring at me. If I were seated in the back middle seat between her and my mother, she would quietly but firmly take my hand and place it in my lap. I wouldn't move it again until I exchanged seats with my sister. Years later when I learned proper nail care and my nails were long and flourishing, I wished I could proudly show them to Mrs. Geleston, but it was too late.

Mother mapped out a rigid itinerary, planning the trip carefully and meticulously budgeting each day's spending from the equal contributions to the spending pool from each of the six. In order to save a night's lodging expense, Mother directed our leaving the farm at 3:00 A.M. Eating peanut butter and crackers in the early morning hours, we stopped few times as we drove across the Mississippi state line and into Tennessee. At noon we stopped beside the highway, unpacking the icebox from the car trunk to enjoy our lunch of fried chicken and pimento cheese sandwiches. The hot air in the car trunk had melted the ice cubes, and our chicken was waterlogged.

Mr. Geleston took a piece of the soaked bird and said, "Watered chicken is pretty good." Nothing was going to hamper our enthusiasm. We had all worked too hard to let such trivial problems dampen our spirits.

As we approached the mountains, our dream came true. The rock cliffs greeted us and appeared like a mirage to us Mississippi Delta flatland folks. How excited we were as we mounted each hill, seeing water rolling along the streams as we wound our way toward the magic of the Smokies.

Our first stop was at a small tourist court outside Chattanooga. We walked around the court and found a restaurant where we ate nickel hamburgers and drank nickel bottled cokes—a meal within our budget. The next morning we rose early and wound our way up Lookout Mountain. Looking through the mounted telescope at the valley and city below, we felt awed by the wonder of the scene.

As we had traveled north, the huge letters painted on barn roofs advertising "See Ruby Falls" had filled us with curiosity, and the excitement increased as we reached the site and prepared to enter. Like characters in an adventure and intrigue novel, we were lowered by a creaking elevator to emerge below the earth's surface. Shivering in the cool air beneath the ground, we followed the slippery narrow path among stalactites and stalagmites, staring at nature's wonders and listening attentively to the tour guide but understanding very little.

After exploring the sights of that area, we followed our carefully orchestrated itinerary to the outskirts of Nashville. We found an air-conditioned tourist court—a retreat from the intense heat of the summer of 1953. The men were impressed by the luxury. We made the first alteration to our plan and stayed two extra nights in the cool comfort.

We found plenty to occupy our time. We toured the Hermitage, home of President Andrew Jackson, and listened to the tour guide tell the history of the beautiful columned home. The setting was a fairy tale, the tall trees, manicured lawns, and flower gardens boasting beautifully blooming begonia and periwinkle. Inside, the polished hardwood floors and canopy beds beckoned us to fantasies of Southern charm and elegance.

In Gatlinburg, we found a small tourist court with a swimming pool and we children were allowed to swim for a short time before supper while our parents and the Gelestons watched us. After supper, my sister and I played "Chinese laundry" in the room we shared with our parents, while the four adults explored the city at night. What fun as we washed our shorts, shirts, and underwear and hung them up to dry all over the bath of the small accommodation. Pretending we ran a laundry, we would talk in make-believe Chinese dialect and spout orders to one another as the pure water flowed over our clothes. How excited we were to see the water clear and clean, with no trace of yellow rust! As the clothes dried the next day, we planned our next game of laundry. That night we unpacked the iron from our suitcase and pressed the clothes, using the bed for an ironing board.

We were sad to leave the beauty of the mountains, but we vowed to return and were encouraged by Mother to start saving our dimes for another trip. But that trip never came.

Today, as I observe my mother enjoying her retirement, hearing her talk of travels to the mountains of Tennessee's Maggie Valley, I know it is well-earned. She still teaches frugality, she still makes endless lists, even though her failing eyesight makes her handwriting almost illegible, and she still teaches traditions that were taught to her.

In turn, my sisters and I pass those traditions to our own children . . . truly, lessons from Mother.

Christmas at Ma-Maw's

Family traditions were taken for granted and as a child I never questioned why some things never changed. Christmas was a time for going to my grandmother's house; for mixing and mingling and sharing with family; for anticipating surprises; and for being happy. All Annie Ethridge's children came to Schlater, Mississippi, and spent Christmas Eve and Christmas Day. Some stayed even longer. The old farmhouse overlooking narrow Lake McNutt would be full of laughter and children. For the grandchildren who gathered from throughout the state, there was a Christmas play to be written and produced, accompanied by music on the out-of-tune piano. It was corny and amateur but the adults encouraged and indulged.

Upon our arrival, the big cedar tree was already decorated with its colored lights shining brightly through the front window to welcome the family home. As each family group arrived, their gifts were added to the growing pile of beautifully wrapped packages under and around the tree. Children would sneak through the curtained french doors into the seldom used and cold living room to count their gifts and shake the boxes to guess their contents.

A cold, informal Christmas Eve supper would be served from the kitchen with the guests sitting wherever a seat could be found. After supper it was time for the Christmas Tree.

While the children and spouses gathered in the living room, Ma-Maw would call her children into her bedroom and pin a hundred-dollar bill on each lapel—their part of the farm's annual crop. Smiles would be on everyone's lips as her children followed Ma-Maw into the living room wearing their money corsages.

Before anything else, one of the older grandchildren would read, "The Night Before Christmas"—an honor every child cherished but only received if Ma-Maw chose you.

Weeks earlier at the Thanksgiving dinner, names had been secretly drawn—the adults from one pile and the children from another. At the Christmas Tree, it was now time to give the gifts and to discover who had drawn your name. Givers and recipients would be announced as the gifts were handed out one by one. Ma-Maw received a gift from each person and she gave everyone a gift. We anxiously watched and waited for treasures to be opened and then passed around for all to see. It took hours. Ma-Maw would insist that all the paper and ribbon be carefully folded and saved for the next year's wrapping. Nothing was wasted.

Before the Christmas Tree, Ma-Maw would secretly ask one of the adults to sneak out during the last moments of the gift opening and rattle bells from the porch. Just as the last gift was passed around, the faint sound of bells was heard, symbolizing the approach of Santa's visit. The children would look at one another wide-eyed with excitement. Ma-Maw would say, "Santa might pass you by if you're still awake. You better hurry." The children would need no more coaxing. Off they would scamper as the sound of bells got closer.

The next morning, the children rose bright and early to discover what Santa had left for each one beside their bed. The stockings had been brought from home and were filled with apples, oranges, and nuts, with playthings on the floor. As the adults drank their coffee in Ma-Maw's bedroom, sharing stories of the year, the children played with Santa's booty. They were mesmerized with the combined volume of trinkets and baubles.

Christmas dinner was a shared effort and took all morning to prepare. Each family brought part of the food. My mother's and her sister's contributions were always the ingredients for ambrosia, a fruit dessert. One would prepare the oranges and the other the coconut, carefully cracking and grating or peeling. In Ma-Maw's kitchen, the two would combine their ingredients to concoct the mixture.

While dinner was cooking, the younger grandchildren entertained themselves with games of "school" on the attic stairs. One child would hold a rock behind her or his back and the other children would guess which hand held the rock. If one successfully guessed, a move to the next step or "grade" was permitted.

When the dinner was ready, Ma-Maw would ring the dinner bell and everyone would come into the dining room for a blessing. Ma-Maw would call on one of the adult men to say the grace and the meal would begin. The table would be covered with a white linen tablecloth and the best china, crystal, and silver would be used along with linen napkins.

The grandchildren were not allowed to eat in the formal dining room; that honor was reserved for adults. In the summer, children ate on the back porch, several sitting on tall green stools and others gathering around the well-worn porch table; but at Christmas we were allowed to eat at the kitchen table and were served from the stove. Children were truly to be seen and not heard, and Ma-Maw insisted that rule be observed.

After the meal of turkey, dressing, corn, peas, stuffed celery, sweet potatoes, pears with cheese, cranberries, and hot rolls, the dessert would immediately be served. Fresh coconut cake, ambrosia, mince meat and pecan pies would be the choices. Everyone would overstuff and fuss because they ate too much.

As the meal ended, each person did his or her part to help clear the table and restore order to the kitchen and dining room. Ma-Maw would leave the chores to her daughters and retire to her bedroom for an after-dinner rest. The children would be directed to play quietly so as not to disturb their grandmother.

People would slowly make their departures in late afternoon, taking plates of food with them. Ma-Maw would kiss and hug each one and stand on the porch waving good-bye. Another Christmas was over and plans had begun for the next family celebration.

Better Than a Covered Dish

The mother of one of my good friends died this week but I had a legitimate excuse not to attend the funeral—I had a meeting. As the day came, the pangs of guilt filled my conscience and I changed my plans.

It's that Southern Baptist upbringing guilt that no one understands unless they had a Ma-Maw who taught that "God will get you if you don't do what's right." And what is right is what she drilled into my impressionable immature soul at a very early age. "When a friend's loved one dies, you fix a covered dish and deliver it, sitting silently close by your friend and holding her hand as she recounts the good times."

The funeral was four hours away in a little Arkansas town, so delivering a covered dish was out of the question. The next best thing would be attending the funeral. Riding that long lonesome road, even with two good friends, would be a dreadful trip. Invited as I had been to come to the house with the other friends and join the family for lunch, it still seemed depressing. I dismissed the thoughts time and time again, only to find them there: What if it were my mother; what if I were four hours from my friends? I felt good; I felt pious; I felt right!

Entering the house was easier than I had imagined. My friend opened the door with a big smile, her sisters were laughing in a corner of the room, her brother seemed more content than usual. There was food—good food. It was a true celebration! There were no tears; there was no morbid mourning; there was only cheerfulness and sincere joy for the life of a 77-year-old woman whom I had not known, but who evidently had touched the lives of so many. The grandchildren kidded each other, the sisters chided, and the in-laws spent their time examining family photographs and asking a lot of questions about half-familiar faces.

The funeral was like many and yet like none, set in a beautiful old funeral home redecorated with cheap paneling, painted windows, and expensive speakers. The odor was a concoction of Pine Sol and Airwick, but the smell was delicious compared to the sound of the out-of-tune piano. Nothing mattered. The seats were full; the walls beside the casket were filled with carefully arranged cut flower sprays that would soon be withering in the scorching June sun on top of a nearby grave. One lone houseplant sat in the corner, symbolizing continuing life—out of place among the blaze of carnations and gladiolus.

The minister I had seen and heard a hundred times and never seen nor heard before. His voice was full of "ye", "thee", and "thou", and the message was memorized and rehearsed utilizing various inflections of the word "good." He didn't know the deceased well, yet he knew her best of all. He was an image of contradiction with his neatly pressed suit and carefully parted hair, standing behind the casket to conceal his notes and speaking distinctly into the hidden microphone. The sound was everywhere. It didn't matter. This was a required ritual and it was over before it began.

Driving home with good friends, feeling very much alive and pleased with life, I knew I had needed today. I needed to know that death is not dying; it is life. Funerals are not for the dead; they are for the living. These people were glad for the time together. They shared experiences, swapped stories, and played "remember when?" The house was lively and full of fun. It was as if I had been there before—as if I knew the faces but not the names.

Ma-Maw would have been proud—even if I didn't bring a covered dish.

Life is a gift
that can be taken away

So live to the fullest—
each and every day.

Time to Divide Iris—Now!

That's what the sign said: "Time to divide iris—now!" I drove by the nursery and tried to imagine how calm life would be if I were concerned about my iris flower beds.

The years have come and gone since I spent hours with delicate blooms. The yellow ones, the purple and white ones —even the variegated species were all-important. I would divide and transplant the bulbs with great care to form a border around the various backyard trees and bird bath. The boys were small and they would help by digging in the dirt or playing ball in the yard.

Life seemed simple and the sign would have been very important then. But today my mind was on other important projects . . . a pre-driver teenage son who needed constant chauffeuring to his many activities in our small town; another son struggling to complete his college education at a local university; my own graduate work yet to complete; computer language to tackle and master; a weary busy husband to help . . . but, most important, a dear sweet friend suffering with terminal cancer. I was afraid the aging thickly-sown iris bulbs thriving in our back yard would have to wait just like the grass and weeds around them. Unlike them, I was juggling, trying hard to survive. I was worried about my friend.

This friend had taught across the hall from me. She was special. The kind of friend you could confess to and celebrate with. She was there for me for twelve years. We stood hall duty together, we sponsored junior-senior proms together, and we worked on floats together. One day she announced that she was quitting teaching.

I said, "Oh, you mean retire."

"No," she said, "I mean quitting. I could teach longer, but I want to quit now and enjoy some years with my husband who is already retired. We like to fish; we have a nice boat and we have enough to live comfortably. He has a heart condition and I want to be with him while I can."

At our school when someone retired, or quit as it was in this case, we would all chip in and buy a gift. My friend didn't mind the gift—in fact she looked forward to it—but her greatest fear was receiving a silver tray.

"You know how I hate cleaning house," she'd explain, "and that special tray with my name engraved with the year I came and the year I left . . . now what good would that do? All it would do is tarnish. I don't want one." She had it all figured out. "I know you'll be collecting the money for the gift and I just want you to know I don't want a tray. See, I've checked on the price of silver trays and I've checked on the price of a piano lamp I want. The lamp is cheaper. I know you can handle it—I want the lamp. I don't want the silver tray."

She had made up her mind. She loved music. She loved to play the piano, and just for herself she purchased a nice one. Now she needed the lamp. It was arranged and she got her lamp. She taught her grandson to play and she sang. She enjoyed those days with her piano and her lamp.

She played, she sang, and she fished for two wonderful years. One day while walking with her husband, she noticed she couldn't move as fast as usual. She consulted the doctor; it was pleurisy. It got no better; she saw a specialist. After several months of visiting specialists, she was diagnosed with cancer of the lining of the lung. It was inoperable.

She lived for two years even though the doctors said she would only have one. She gave it all she had right up to the end. She lost her hair but bought a wig, and she kept on fishing and playing bridge with her friends. During the last few months, she continued to have that same spark of life. She gave a message to those of us she left behind. We have good memories of her— because she truly celebrated the temporary. Now my friend was dying. I was staying with her for the night. How badly I wished I could recapture those quiet days of backyard digging and play. How simple my life was then. My friend was once also worried about her iris. She and I worked hard—always planning for the future . . . those glorious days when the chores would be done and we could sit and visit guiltlessly. Those days never came. There were more and more chores; the children grew; her grandchildren replaced them in priority. We shared little quality time with each other. We were always accomplishing; always eager to divide the iris. What a tragedy! The iris will wait. They'll be back. Maybe a little thicker, maybe not as pretty, maybe even less than perfect, but they'll be back. My friend won't!

Thinning gray strands of hair clung to her forehead as she struggled for precious air. It was difficult to imagine this source of creative energy and unlimited strength reduced to this dependent state. But even in her illness, even in the last days of struggle, she visually and verbally redecorated the hospital room and gave orders to her friends who acted as sitters. In the final hours, she refused to eat—locking her lips and shaking her head violently from side to side. She wanted to die; she desired release from the pain. She was ready, resigned to the end. She was content to pass from this world. Those of us who stood by her bedside pleading with her to take nourishment knew it was a futile attempt.

She had always been the strong one—listening to our concerns, our needs, offering needed advice and counsel on issues from knitting to bridge to classroom teaching skills. Now we attempted to repay her with unsolicited advice and counsel and she remained staunch in her refusal to obey. I clutched her hand and begged her to try to eat but she turned her head. What a difference two years can make. I remembered the strong, dedicated teacher who stood at her door proudly between class periods, reminding exiting students of their assignments and welcoming those entering with reminders, "Assignment is on the board; make sure you have it ready."

I remembered her efficient and effective work as a class sponsor, department chairperson, and classroom instructor. Why? Why this waste of talent? Why should she be a needless victim? Why her? She wanted so badly to live. She tried so hard to fight the illness that now consumed her body. Her bloated face and protruding abdomen told the tale of hours of needed chemotherapy. I thought of how we laughingly had joked about liposuction for our sagging tummies just a few years earlier. I remembered her practice of holding shoulders erect to camouflage the problem. I thought of the walking program we planned and executed faithfully.

Now she was leaving me—content to pass to the hereafter without winning this war with cancer. It wasn't fair nor was it meant to be. She was ready, eager for the end of struggle. There was no bitterness in her voice, no hostility in her words. She had made peace; it was to be over soon and she welcomed it. It was I and those left behind who were bitter and hostile.

Her words were quiet and simple as she gasped for breath with her newly-installed oxygen apparatus. "I wish I could have gone on a cruise—maybe I will." Then she looked up at me—felt for my nearby hand and touched my fingers and asked, "Do you think I will?"

She made statements and asked questions all at once. What could I say to this frail failing friend? Life seemed irrelevant, nothing seemed important but breathing life back into her feeble body.

I gently squeezed her hand and said, "Sure you will." Tears streamed down her cheeks. She knew I was lying. It was our last visit for conversation.

Now it's August again and the sign is back up. "Time to divide iris— now!" I didn't divide the iris this year either.

My friend Bettye is dead and I miss her terribly. Instead of grieving, I called and invited a mutual friend for coffee and we relived some cherished memories of our Bettye. As we sat on my back screened porch, I could see the badly neglected iris below but I felt no guilt as I sipped my coffee. I did feel disappointment that I had spent so much time dividing the iris in years past and less time with friends. But at last I realize the importance of celebrating friendships in the here and now— of knowing that iris can wait—but people can't.

STORIES

of School and Church

Empty Eyes and Stomachs

Some time ago, I served as the sponsor of our church youth. One September we began talking and discussing the plight of church missions and one of our youth asked if we could actually take part in a mission trip. The answer was a resounding "Yes."

After much investigation, we discovered that a foreign mission trip was an expensive endeavor and one that would take much time and effort—more time and money than our small church had to give. We must do something; the youth were anxious to serve. But we were small; we had nine youth aged 13 to 17. What could we do for missions?

We read about an effort in a city five hours from our home. This mission was housed in a large church in the center of downtown and had been operating for several years. The church invited youth groups to come and spend a week serving stew to the homeless street people and operating an afternoon daycare activity center in the church. Was this our answer to a mission trip?

We all agreed it was and spent months preparing ourselves for the week of service. We found out rather quickly that we knew very little about working with the less fortunate. We knew nothing about geriatrics, alcoholics, the homeless, drug abusers, and other inner city problems. We were protected by our white middle-class values and standards and had not been anxious to explore the magnitude of the problems. Our concern had been confined to attending Sunday School and reading mission magazines.

We wrote our questions and answered them at the same time.

"Would the people in the mission be old or young; men or women?"

Definitely old, we decided; both men and women.

"Would they be black or white or maybe even 'other'?"

Probably black, maybe white, but certainly nothing like us.

"Would they want help or would they just be there for a free meal?"

Surely they were simply losers because after all, we had been taught that any man or woman could pull himself or herself "up by the bootstraps" if they were really determined.

We had another major question for which we had no answer: "Could we be missionaries in the shadow of a metropolitan area that houses a fabulous shopping and fashion area, a nationally famous zoo, and a fun and lively theme park?"

One thirteen-year-old asked, "How much time will we have to have fun?"

During the year we collected as much information as we could. We invited guest speakers from nearby colleges to share their expertise on drug abuse and old age. We learned CPR. We read and we educated ourselves but it was not enough.

The months flew by and we knew a lot of facts but we had no practical experience. Our local church was supportive and donated $500 to our cause. We sponsored a Mexican Dinner, cooking and serving the food to raise over $300 more. We organized our schedule and detailed duty charts. We planned our menus and decided our free time entertainment. We rented a van; we packed our clothes; we made lists of things to do. So much work for so little time, we thought.

We arrived in the city late one Sunday afternoon. We found the church and we circled and gawked. Such a large building, massive with its city-block large brick facade and gold-domed sanctuary. Nestled in the concrete were green and lush court-yards leading to covered doorways.

Two of our group screamed simultaneously, "Look, a wino!"

With that exclamation, we all glanced at a courtyard entrance to see a dirty ill-kempt man stagger along the brick wall between the church and the street. In his hand was a well-worn brown paper sack. We looked at one another in disbelief. This was real; this was our mission field and we were scared. We had seen winos before. We had all driven along the river in a nearby town and we had seen the homeless under the bridges. We had even seen one or two in our own little town of 10,000. But the difference was clear—this man would be at our table in the morning and we would be expected to serve him food. He was our mission. It was too late to go home.

From the first time the door to the parking garage which housed the mission was opened and we smelled the stench, until the last day when the youth picked up the last bowl to wash, it was a test in perseverance. Our questions had been answered.

Most of the street people were younger than expected, most were men and the majority were white. Some were hand-icapped. One paraplegic was a pathetic case, living on the pub-lic buses at night until the route shut down, being wheeled into the bushes of a public park, where he would stay until morn-ing. The youth were repulsed by the number of insect bites on his body. He gave a different name every day.

The people carried everything they owned on their backs. They had no homes. Some wanted to work, but mental and emotional problems kept them on the street. Others were runa-ways. Most did not stray far from this church—their refuge and guaranteed daily hot meal.

We were over-prepared. These homeless souls didn't need CPR; they didn't desire counseling. All they wanted was a place out of the hot sun, a hot meal, and someone to listen to untrue stories when they cared to talk. They offered no explanations for their plights, no last names and no apologies for their dirty state.

After serving the hot bowls of soup or stew, we would return to our kitchen to eat our noon meal. It was difficult. We had little appetite. We found ourselves looking forward to the children in the day-care center who were appreciative and longed for a smile and touch from our youth. These unfortunate lived on the streets around their homes with only the concrete sidewalks for a playground. The hot lunch coupled with lessons with clay, music, and games was a reprieve from the heat and harsh reality of their ghetto neighborhood.

One of our girls suggested an outing to a park on our last day. Simple joys took on new meaning as our group pushed swings and merry-go-rounds with laughter.

The last night as we returned to the church after eating out, we circled the building to see the police arresting one of the people that we had served every day. "Oh, no," one of the group shouted. "They're taking away Charlie."

How a week had changed their attitudes. No longer would they only read about missions in a book, they had experienced the pain and joy in caring for those less fortunate. Though they would return to their middle-class values, they would never take them for granted again. It was a week they would never forget.

The S.T.A.F.F. Meetings

Morale was rock bottom in the small school district; the teachers had no reason to hope it would improve. The low self-esteem was affecting that of the students and the entire town was suffering. There was little money for teacher raises and needed building improvements were not possible. Faculty members griped in daily huddles. Teachers didn't feel anyone was really listening to their problems. They were not consulted on solutions and possibilities that affected teaching conditions and learning. There were faculty meetings but they compounded the problem. They offered little promise for solving the dilemma. There seemed to be no answer.

One day a creative and energetic teacher spoke with some teacher friends, "We need to meet outside the school to discuss our week's work—talk candidly about our problems and discuss solutions. We need no ultimatums; no planned agenda—just time to enjoy one another's support. We've got to stop the moaning and groaning."

Several teachers agreed and it was decided that each Friday afternoon the group would meet at someone's home. The week's activities would be discussed and time together would be enjoyed. Teachers would come as soon as they could get away from school at the end of the day. They would stay as long as they chose. After their meeting, the weekend would be better because the negative thoughts would be diluted.

Teacher spouses would be invited too.

"Let's try it and see," she urged as she offered to have the meeting at her house.

It was a success. By the fourth week, all district buildings were represented. There was laughter and fun, good food and conversation. It made a difference. On Monday, those who had attended felt better equipped to face the week. It seemed to be the answer to morale problems.

Every Friday, someone volunteered to host the next staff meeting. The word would spread. Phones would ring and messages would be sent, "Staff meeting today at Sue's."

In the beginning the meetings were somewhat negative as teachers recounted their frustrations and concerns. But as the group continued to meet, trust was developed and friendships bonded. The negative experiences still caused heartache and even pain, but sharing them helped the teachers to learn from each other.

They concentrated on choices. They would be reminded to stay in the present, not to rehash the past, and to dismiss worry about the future. The group realized they had the power to inspire each other.

No one was denied admittance. A few times, even an administrator might drop by. There were no secrets; there were no surprises. Daily encounters were recalled and laughter filled the room. The jokes were personal and willingly shared.

At times, there might be serious philosophical discussions with some debate and perhaps disagreement. All the conversation was educational and inspirational.

After several years, some of the ideas and goals that sprang from this group were realized. Several spouses took the problems to heart and ran for the local school board and won. The district began to rise above its problems. A tax hike was approved by the voters, buildings were repaired and remodeled, salaries were improved, and student test scores were better.

Even now in the little town, on some Friday afternoons after a hectic week, you can hear a veteran teacher say, "It's time for a STAFF meeting."

"Staff meeting?" a new teacher will ask. "The last thing I need is another meeting."

A veteran Staffer will respond, "Then you will love this staff meeting. Staff stands for Society for Teacher Advocates for Friday Frolicking."

To Achieve . . .
You've Got To Believe!

Times Have Changed

When my sister and I were little, we'd talk about what we wanted to be when we finally grew up. Dolls and teddy bears would mirror our dreams. Our first aspirations were "When I get big . . . " or "When I grow up . . . "

"When I get big, I'll be a teacher just like Mrs. Walker or Mrs. McCord or Mrs. Dorris," I would say as I named my current teacher.

At other times, I would want to be like my Mother's sisters. They were both schoolteachers in other towns. I'd say, "I'll be just like my Aunt Margaret or my Aunt Sallye Hunt."

My sister and I would play paper dolls and when my sister's "Mommy" went off to work, it was as a nurse. My "Mommy" was a teacher. I lined up dolls and teddy bears on my bed and I played school for hours in my room.

I lived in the country, but I went to the city school. Some of my neighbors went to the country school and that school was closed during part of the year because of the work in the fields. As I got older, I would get off the bus and after the country school children had finished their work and I finished my chores, we would play school. I would teach my playmates every lesson I had learned that day.

I don't see many children playing school today. Little ones play make believe and they talk about their future jobs, but few of them are talking about being teachers. Parents may not encourage them to teach and and even if they do, they don't talk about it in public.

When the children are older, they may say, "I may teach, if things don't work out in another area."

One day I attended an academic competition for gifted and talented students and observed my son in the final rounds of group problem-solving. When he had finished his part on the program, one of his teachers turned to me and said, "Your son is a very talented young man. I know you are very proud." She explained, "He speaks well in public, he articulates, he works hard, and he is a born leader."

I beamed with pride as she asked, "What does he want to be?"

I thought about all those wonderful qualities and said, "Well, maybe one day he will be a teacher."

She looked at me, puzzled and with a wrinkled brow, and said, "Oh, no, he's smarter than that."

Shortly after that encounter, I attended a reunion at my home church in the community where I grew up. I was visiting with a friend when a former Sunday School teacher asked my friend about her life.

"What are you doing?" asked the teacher.

My friend responded, "I'm a kindergarten teacher."

"I'll bet you are a good one," the Sunday School teacher said.

My friend responded, "I really am! I love teaching!"

What a difference in those two encounters. The attitude denominator is awesome. The teacher of gifted and talented students had an awesome responsibility and opportunity for influencing the brightest and best in our community, but she was not convinced of the worth of educators and the esteem of the teaching profession. If her students wanted to be teachers, they would not be encouraged. They would apologize.

The kindergarten teacher believed in her profession; believed in her own ability; believed in herself. She knew that if she believed in her profession, her ability, and herself that others would also. She was convincing the public that teaching is an honorable profession.

Not only did she believe in her own abilities, but she spoke of her belief in the abilities of her colleagues. She supported them and they believed in each other. Because of this loyalty, others supported and believed in the faculty and the school.

Her attitude at the church homecoming was contagious. The young people were interested in her teaching experiences. We've got to be more like that kindergarten teacher. We must promote the teaching profession and recruit the brightest and the best to join us in the marvelous experience of teaching and learning.

A Diamond in the Rough

I taught special students. Those that could but would not try to learn or behave were hustled off to our classroom. When I first started in the late 60's, there were few guidelines and regulations and no public laws. I was given students for a day, a month, or year and told to teach; to cure the problem. There were few materials for the slower learner, fewer dollars, and most of the students dropped out before finishing high school. I wanted it to be different.

Moving to another state and armed with experience in special education, I was assigned as teacher in a federally-funded Title program. I was the third teacher in three years. We were placed in the older part of the lower elementary building, separate from other classes, teachers, and regular students. Another class for the handicapped and the school counselor shared our building. Our students were all grade levels and we bused them to our room for segments of instruction. The students were what we would term today "learning disabled." Most were bright—some were even gifted, but all had one commonality: they were not achieving in the regular classroom.

Our days were spent with nontraditional learning— individualized motivational activities. We worked on academics, but our main objective was attitude adjustment. We would reward exemplary behavior and academic achievement with points every day.

Every Friday, we set up our "Point Store." Scattered on the reading table would be all sorts of goodies: food, jewelry, gifts, school supplies. Whatever we and others donated, we put into our store. The students never knew from one week to the next what treasures we would present. Every item was given a point value.

The eager students would bring their point sheets to the store and "buy" whatever they wanted. Sometimes we offered a special: a trip to get an ice cream cone or a field trip to a nearby museum, a park. The store had layaway and gift wrapping—all for a charge of points. We also featured a bank where students could deposit their points if they saw nothing they wanted that week.

All the students were different with varying needs, but they had one thing in common: none of the students thought they were important. They could learn, sure, but they didn't believe they could because they had been told for so long they were slow. The system had passed them by. They were not respected by their peers and the teachers didn't want them in their class. Most were considered troublemakers.

Jimmy was like the rest, but with an added disadvantage: he was a foster child. He was 13 years old and had been in nine foster homes. He was taller than the other boys his age, slumping his shoulders when he stood so he wouldn't tower above them. He caused problems in the classroom, in the hall, on the playground—wherever he went. He didn't want to work; he said he didn't understand, though he did. He wanted the teacher's special attention. The teacher was tired of Jimmy. She had 30 other students to worry about and she called Jimmy "stubborn and hostile." She told him the class was better when he was absent. He helped her by staying home whenever he could. He ended up in our program.

Jimmy didn't need worksheets. He didn't need drills. The counselor told us that what he did need was a boost of confidence; he needed to believe in himself. We were his prescription.

He had been in our program several months and we had made little progress. He sulked when asked to do his work; he couldn't be trusted to do any homework and he would steal from other students. He was a misfit; he had no friends. He told everyone he wouldn't be with us long; the social worker would come one day and he would be carted off to another foster home in another city. Why should he try? We were determined that as long as he was with us, we wouldn't give up.

We told Jimmy that if he would earn fifty behavior and work points he could choose a trip and we would offer it to the students in the "Point Store." Jimmy didn't believe us. Many people had promised Jimmy things, but few had delivered.

"You mean we can go anywhere?" he quizzed us.

"Within reason, yes. It has to be educational and it has to be within an hour of the school," I said. "Where do you want to go?"

Jimmy thought for a moment, cocked his head and sarcastically snarled, "I want to hunt diamonds. They used to call me Diamond Jim at the Home."

We lived near a State Park that boasted a diamond mine. I assured him that going was a possibility.

"Do you know about how to find diamonds, Jimmy?" I asked, seeing that the other students were interested in the trip.

"I heard about it at the children's home one time," he said proudly, trying to impress his peers.

"Well, Jimmy, you earn your points next week and we'll plan a trip," I promised.

Not sure how the principal would react, I determined that if he earned the points, we would make the trip. She agreed that anything was worth a try. "Jimmy's been on everybody's bad list, you know. I don't think he'll do it." She shrugged. "It's worth a try, but don't be disappointed."

The principal was a veteran; she had had all kinds. She was the type administrator that gave you a list of problem students at the first of the year, recited the rules to everyone, and required that you have a ten-cent whistle with you at all times. She allowed no foolishness; even touching walls on the way to the rest room was forbidden. Jimmy was a thorn in her side.

All week, everyone encouraged Jimmy. Other students prodded him to do his work. He was their trip ticket and his behavior and work took on new meaning to all of us. He didn't miss a day all week—quite a record for Jimmy.

While the store had been a strong motivator for the other students, Jimmy had never been interested in any of it. He would use his few weekly points for an apple or pieces of candy and spend it all. He had no points in the bank like the other students.

On Friday, the aide counted Jimmy's point sheet first. "Forty-eight points, Jimmy. Not quite enough." The most that Jimmy had ever received was twenty-one, so we were pleased, but Jimmy was not.

He negotiated, "I have a paper I haven't handed in. It's worth five points. Is it too late?" he pleaded.

"Not if you have it completed," I said.

Jimmy raced to his notebook, found the paper, and presented it to me. It was perfect. He had more than the fifty points.

"O.K., Jimmy. We'll feature a trip to the diamond mine in the store tomorrow. It will cost fifty points," I said.

Friday came and we opened the store. There were some interesting items. A friend of mine had cleaned out her son's toy box and donated a sack of usable toys.

We had coupons for the diamond trip—enough for every student. Each student quickly bought the trip. Jimmy sat at his desk. He glanced over his shoulder at the set of miniature metal cars for 30 points. He knew he couldn't have both.

Carefully he walked up and down the table that was our portable store. He handled several cars. He was tantalizing the other students. Finally he pulled a coupon from the table, handing me his point sheet.

The other students clapped and yelled.

We were going to the diamond mine and everyone seemed excited. We scheduled the trip for the following week.

It had worked. We had one good week of work and effort from Jimmy. But it didn't last. Monday he was absent. Our practice was to go to the homes to check on students when they didn't show up.

"Jimmy's bad sick," the foster mother told the aide. "But he'll be there tomorrow to go on that trip."

Bright and early, we boarded our van and left for the diamond mine. It was my first experience at diamond hunting so I was as excited as the students.

All the way, Jimmy sat in the back of the van and acted ugly. He pinched Karen and he shoved Chad. He was unimpressed with the pretty scenery and told everyone he had seen it all before.

"Come on, Jimmy, start over here with me," I offered after we had paid our admission fee and received our digging tools.

"Nah, this is stupid. I thought it would be a real mine. Why this is nothing but an old field," Jimmy scoffed. "Can I sit in the van and listen to the radio?"

"Absolutely not!" I insisted, almost losing my patience in the hot sun and thinking but not saying, 'Look, Buster, this was your big idea and you are going to dig and enjoy it like everyone else.'

After an hour of unsuccessful sifting through the dirt, the students were bored and tired. Jimmy sat on the sloping field, drawing figures with a stick.

I made my way toward him saying, "O.K. boys and girls. Are you ready for this? Jimmy and I are going to show you just how easy it is to find a diamond."

With that exclamation, I kneeled down beside Jimmy and began to pull the dirt back with my hands, putting clumps of sod in the tray. Jimmy sat and stared at the ground.

"I'll tell you what, honey," I whispered my offer. "Just because you're Diamond Jim, we'll be partners. If we find a diamond, we'll go halves."

"That ain't how you do it," Jimmy said. "Want me to show you?"

With that, he reached down, grabbed a big piece of sod and sifted through it with his fingers. I watched him and did the same.

"Look at this, Jimmy. I found a diamond," I kidded as I placed a tiny minuscule pebble in the palm of my hand for him to see.

Jimmy looked at it and asked, "That's a diamond?"

Wanting to excite him and motivate the other children, I pretended, "I think so. I'll put it in my sack and we'll see when we go out. Remember the lady said diamonds in the rough don't shine. They're not polished."

By this time the entire group was gathered around and beginning to dig in our spot. Before you knew it, we were all laughing and talking about our "diamonds."

As we left the park an hour later, I almost forgot about the pebble in my sack, but Jimmy hadn't. "Show her your diamond," he said as he motioned for me to open my sack.

The lady said, "Let me see," and took the sack from me, shaking out the contents on the counter and putting her eyepiece on.

"Yes, you have a nice little diamond there," she said, caressing the little pebble.

"What?" all the students yelled and crowded around.

"It's not very big and it will cost you more than it's worth to have it polished, but yes, it is a diamond. It's what we call a chip."

"Gosh, Jimmy, if you hadn't showed me how to hunt diamonds, I would never have found this," I said. "Aren't you glad you came. And to think, you own half of this."

"How much is it worth?" he asked the lady.

"About $10 like that," she answered. "But we don't buy them."

Jimmy figured in his head, "Can I just have the $5?" he asked me.

"Sure!" I said, "But are you sure you wouldn't rather have the diamond?"

"I don't want no diamond that little. I'd just lose it. I want the money."

Armed with his $5, he rode proudly home, announcing to everyone that he knew more about diamond hunting than anybody in the school. And he did.

He was never the same after our trip to that dusty hot field. He walked taller and he stood prouder. We called him Diamond Jim and he beamed. We kept the little diamond in my desk wrapped in a tissue and every now and then he would ask to see it to show it to a new student. In time, it disappeared.

Just as he predicted, at the end of the semester, a social worker came and checked Jimmy out of school. He promised to write to us and let us know where he lived. He didn't. We never knew what happened to Jimmy. He left our school bound for yet another foster home.

You Mean I Can't
Call Them Darling?

For years, as an elementary and secondary teacher and a school administrator, I called my students loving, endearing terms like Darling, Honey, and Sweetheart. It didn't matter who they were or how big they were, they all got the same treatment. Today, when I see these students they are adults, many with children of their own, but they still might be called Darling, Honey, or Sweetheart.

Recently, I read a newspaper story about a principal at an inner city school being chastised for calling students "Honey."

I found the story interesting because in the same newspaper was an article on student self-esteem. A psychologist was warning that schoolteachers and school administrators need to show more caring and love to the students. "Our students need to know that they have a friend at school."

In 1973, the Federal Title Special Education Program I had taught at the elementary school was eliminated for lack of funds. I was transferred to the local high school to teach special education. The class was entitled "Work Study Experience Program" because the students were allowed to do academics part of the day and work in the community several hours each day. The program had been housed at the elementary school for several years, but the parents were complaining because the students were high school age and on a campus with first graders. It was degrading for them to eat in the lunchroom and sit in the primary chairs. Reluctantly, the administration agreed to allow the program to be housed at the new one-year-old high school building.

Before school began, I showed up at the school eager to ready my room for the year. The principal was noticeably upset with our program being on his campus,

"We don't have room, you know," he warned. "I don't know where we'll put you. How many students do you have?"

I admitted that I didn't know but was told it wouldn't be more than 15.

"Fifteen! I know we don't have room for that many," he said scornfully. "What do they expect me to do?"

I assured him that I had no suggestions. It was my first visit to the building. I walked behind him as he mumbled about the lack of planning. My excitement waned as he complained.

"Don't you have a small classroom?" I begged. "I understand the students are really looking forward to being with their age group. You know, they've been with first-graders." I tried to persuade without arguing. This man would be my new boss and I wanted to get off on the right foot.

"All we have is this," he said, taking out his key and opening a door behind the stage. The sign outside said "Dressing Room."

I tried not to laugh. He was serious. "This is the best I can do."

The room was bare with painted concrete block walls and tile floors. At the other end was a door leading to the back of the stage of the little theater. Like all classrooms in the building, it had no windows. I was discouraged. How could this be a classroom?

The principal promised desks for the students and hopefully he could find one for me. He left me there to contemplate my dilemma. I walked down the halls of the school, trying to acquaint myself with the building. The classrooms were beautiful, equipped with brightly colored desks, wooden storage cabinets, and carpet.

"Maybe I can manage," I promised myself as I walked to my car to unload my boxes of salvaged supplies from the Federal program.

I stacked everything against a wall, went by the principal's office, and gave him a small list of needed items. "Just the essentials," I apologized. "Student and teacher desks, chalk board, bulletin board," I read from the list. "I'll be back later in the week."

For several days, I sorted through the supplies and remainders of the program at the elementary school, trashing anything that was juvenile and unsuitable for high school students. That left very little material.

When I returned to the high school, the principal was unavailable. The custodian opened the room, still clearly marked, "Dressing Room." Inside had been crammed 15 arm desks, old and worn, evidently saved from the old high school building. A small, scarred, wooden, teacher desk and chair were out in the hall. They would not fit in the room. There was no bulletin or chalk board.

I organized the room with eight desks, placing the others in the area outside the stage door. Bringing in the dilapidated teacher desk, I cleaned out the drawers and organized my essential supplies. I sat in the worn chair feeling discouraged as splinters scratched my legs.

"It's not fair," I thought angrily. "But what can I do? I'm new to the school and to the town. I don't know the students or the parents. I have to manage somehow. I have to make this work." I rationalized that the students and their parents would be so glad to just be on the high school campus that they would not care about the classroom.

I went to the office to get schedules. I had 13 students and each schedule read the same: "Special Education."

"We don't have them in any other classes," the principal explained. "We didn't know they were going to be here. Maybe after school starts, we can put them somewhere."

"Somewhere!" I thought. "These are human beings, not

animals." But I decided to anger him would serve no purpose. I would have to convince him to make changes, but it would take time.

For several days I worked in the little closet that was to be my home for the next nine months. Over the "Dressing Room" sign I taped a piece of paper which read: Work Study Experience Program. I taped colored paper to the concrete walls and taped letters to it which read: WELCOME BACK! I made a "mailbox" for each student, carefully lettering their names on each and taping them on the back of the stage door. Inside I placed their schedules and an information sheet about our program. I brought a bookcase from home and arranged the assortment of materials in a corner. The room was now more crowded. How would we all fit?

I carefully studied the class schedule and the students' folders, attempting to find classes into which I could mainstream the students. I met some of the teachers who were working in their rooms. Most seemed glad we were to be a part of the high school program, but some seemed to resent us. Clearly we were viewed as unwelcome intruders.

During registration days, the students began to drop by to investigate their new home. I tried to be positive. "We'll use the area outside the stage door if this gets too crowded," I promised. One by one I met them. They were so different but with one thing in common. They were scared. Instead of being glad to be at the high school campus with their peer group, they were concerned and embarrassed. They confided that maybe we would be better off to return to the elementary school where we had a larger room and everyone knew us. They didn't say it, but I could see on their faces a fear of me. They missed their teacher. They wanted familiar territory.

"Oh, no," I insisted. "This will be much better."

But even I wasn't sure and the days that followed confirmed my doubts. We were clearly in the way. As the days progressed, it was difficult to convince many of the faculty to allow the students to attend their classes. The home economics teacher was wonderful; she welcomed them into any of her classes. All of them were placed in remedial reading and physical education classes. Some of them were placed in beginning typing and two were allowed to attend the basic science class.

Even though the principal suggested that we eat earlier than the other students to avoid adding to the already heavy lunch traffic, I convinced him that this was unfair to my students. We wanted to be with the other students.

Every morning first period all the students would meet for a class in Vocational Skills. We would sit in the little theater seats and we would talk about job skills: interviewing, application forms, attitude—anything that would help them to gain and keep employment. But jobs were hard to find. Several found jobs on their own baby-sitting and doing yard work on weekends, but there were few jobs for them during the school week.

As part of the program, we were assigned a counselor from the state Rehabilitation Services. She came to see us once each week. Each time she arrived, I had a list of suggested employers for her to contact and students to help.

The Rehabilitation Counselor told me about funds available for training jobs on campus. We carefully listed various jobs our students could perform. They could certainly serve food in the cafeteria and wash dishes; they could clean the tables and sweep the floor. They could help the custodians. After meeting with the principal and assuring him that it would be a help to the school in labor and funds, we were given permission to talk with the District Food Supervisor. She was very helpful and agreed to let the students work on a trial basis. We were so excited.

Every day before lunch, six carefully selected students would go to the cafeteria and eat early with the lunchroom workers, donning their aprons and hairnets for work during the busy lunch period. Four served food and two worked in the dishroom operating the washing machines. They were appreciated by the lunchroom staff, and by the end of the year the supervisor agreed that we could add another slot in the dishroom. The students were paid minimum wage with half the money coming from the District and the other half from Rehabilitation Services. It was cheap labor for the District and the salvation of our program. When the students would receive their checks, they would be so proud. Some of the regular students made fun of them and would call them "Retarded," and although it certainly hurt feelings, the students endured the pain for the work experience and the money. We discussed the insults and we supported one another. Everyone was important.

Slowly, we convinced several businesses in town to hire our students on a trial basis. We discovered grants to help with training. We were making slow progress but most of the students still had little academic knowledge and no work skills.

We worked hard; some stayed after school and I would take them home. Many came early, sitting in the desks on the dimly lighted area off stage. They had few friends outside our program. They felt secure in our area. Discipline problems were few. We were too busy. We crammed so much work into so little time. Every paper was returned in their mailboxes and had to be corrected before the students received credit. Completed papers were carefully organized in notebooks by subjects. We taught it all: vocational skills, math, English, social studies. Whatever the students needed, we offered.

Shortly before the Christmas vacation, the local college called and asked if I would accept a practicum social worker as an intern. "Of course," I eagerly accepted. "We would love to have the help." It was set for the intern to begin after the holidays. I made lists of duties for her. She would help organize a manual for our program and aid in helping find jobs.

By spring, the football coach was talking to several of our guys about going out for the team. The intern and Rehabilitation Counselor had found jobs for every student originally in the program and we were checking on them weekly.

Students were added to our program. We had 18 by the end of the year. Several were sent to us with a note about behavior problems or fights. We took them all. We kept them the rest of the year.

By February, we had convinced the principal to allow us to expand into the women's restroom. We needed an office for the Rehabilitation Counselor to counsel the students. The restroom was small with a slanted tile floor with a center drain. It adjoined a smaller room housing the commode and sink. It didn't look like an office and the sign outside said "Women."

A friend was having a garage sale and selling some old carpet from her house. The local Civitan Club agreed to buy the carpet for us. It cost $15. The assistant principal helped me and we cut and glued the carpet to the tile floor. We moved the teacher desk and bookcase into the new "office." We taped motivational posters on the walls and charts of student achievement.

We rearranged our classroom with a small table and the

student desks. It was dark between the restroom and our classroom, and often between classes regular students would hide behind the stage curtain and heckle my students as they worked. At times, the band would set up on the stage and we couldn't have class. When there was an assembly, we would attend once, returning to the closet to hear it again because the size of the student body demanded that every assembly be repeated.

We asked the school counselor and principal to arrange mock interviews with our students to discuss job goals and future plans. Both agreed and seemed shocked that these misfits would be able to contribute anything to our community.

"Just talk to them," I pleaded. "Ask them questions and see if they can respond. They need the experience."

At the end of the year, two of our students were ready to graduate. They were ready. In addition to their basic academic skills, they had learned to complete various application forms; they could respond appropriately in an interview; they could balance a checkbook, complete an IRS short form, and they were registered to vote. They had held jobs in the cafeteria and been placed in jobs in the community. We had a graduation party for them complete with balloons and cake. We were sad to see them leave us. In that dressing room and women's restroom, we had become a family.

So please excuse me while I call my students Darling.

You've got a lot to give–
don't go it alone.

Just remember–
you can rest when you
get to the nursing home.

Boring—Really Boring

My friend, the school librarian, said we were boring; in fact she really said "old and boring." She was over 50 and was one of those unusual friends who says what she means and means what she says.

We'd been friends a long time—the three of us. We shared many commonalities, but we understood our distinct differences, too. We were schoolteachers in the same district. Our children had attended the local schools. We'd laughed and cried together many times. We'd shared celebrations and sadness. We had been activists, vitally interested in our profession. We had taken part in community activities as well as school reform. We had worked together in political campaigns and civic efforts. We agreed on many issues, but were close enough to learn to disagree. We shared our feelings without fear of reprisal. We had years of experiences that bonded us together.

But those years of activism seemed long ago and far away. We were more comfortable now. We had few battles to fight; no wars to win.

"All we used to talk about was school," Sue explained. "Now, we might talk about our yards and flowers and often we'll mention our grown children, or how we need to exercise, but basically we are boring! Really boring!"

She got our attention. We were all listening. Even the spouses gathered around. "We need a club," she explained.

"Something to make us plan fun and really carry out the plan. We can't work all the time and expect life to be a joy. We have to create little celebrations."

And so, convinced that we were boring—old and boring— the CEOC or "Couples Eating Out Club" was born. It was decided that we would meet one weekend a month—nothing structured; it can be any time during the month and we would rotate the duty of planning a night out. Not really an unusual idea except that the person in charge would secretly plan the destination and the agenda, being responsible for all the plans.

"God forbid," she said, "one of you might actually want to cook a dinner at your house." She agreed to not only head up the club but to host the first meeting. The destination was secret and the dress casual.

We drove out of town to a nearby tourist area. It was a new restaurant and they were expecting us. The food was scrumptious, but the important ingredient was the fact that we were committed to fun—even only once a month. In her toast Sue recognized that commitment when she mused:

> Wouldn't it be quite awful
>   if all your friends were just like you?
> They'd close their drapes and cabinet doors
>   and sit in a specially marked church pew.
> They'd put their capped toothpaste tubes
>   in carefully marked places.
> Their politics would not sway to the left
>   or right with any special cases.
> The laughter would be convenient;
>   But never roaring;
> Thoughts and actions would be the same—
>   Boring!
> But then we're different! Thank goodness!
>   Why, look at us gathered here tonight.
> All with differing backgrounds—even ages;
>   We offer bits of strangeness and delight.

We disagree; we argue;
    We are not the same!
Even in religious discussions,
    We call no names.
We generate excitement
    From books we read to songs we've sung,
From places we've been to places we're going,
    Sticking together we'll be forever young.
Never boring!

Under Her Wing

It was my first teaching assignment. My husband was a Navy man and we were stationed on the east coast in a little town on the Delaware Bay. I needed to work. Armed with my teaching credentials and a year of social work experience, I set out to find a job. After many fruitless hours and days, I was finally offered a job as a fourth grade teacher at an elementary school in a nearby town. The school building was old but well kept, and my room was to be on the front with tall ceilings and big windows. I worked hours cleaning and polishing to make it just right for my thirty-two eager and promising students.

The year started and at the first faculty meeting, the principal assigned each of the new teachers a big sister or big brother—a tenured, experienced teacher to serve as guide and adviser to novices. My big sister was a beautiful lady named Marguerite White. She was teaching her last year and I was teaching my first. What a beautiful combination. She carefully showed me how to keep the attendance register, lesson plans, and how to supplement the textbooks with creative activities. She shared all her materials with me and helped me find others. I watched her in her daily activities—lunch count, homeroom parties, playground duty, field trips, unit lessons. I marveled at her ability to make it all fit. Every activity she tied into a lesson. She was retiring, but she taught that last year just like it was her first.

Teaching across the hall from her was the best lesson of all. I learned how to motivate; how to discipline; how to teach—from Marguerite. But perhaps more often, I learned valuable lessons about loyalty and trust, team teaching, and sharing friendships.

Marguerite appreciated antiques and her home was full of treasures from her family. Every piece of furniture and every trinket had a story that would carefully unfold as she stroked the chair or piece of glass. The stories were priceless lessons in Delaware and Maryland history. She took me to the local antique dealers and she taught me lessons on collecting and identification of wood and glassware. When my husband worked on weekends, Marguerite and I would comb the countryside looking for bargains. I learned the lessons well. She was a good teacher.

She was also an artist—a painter. Late in adulthood, after her husband's death, she had taken lessons from a local artist. A dedicated student, she would pack up her art tools and go to the beach or the woods and sit for hours sketching and painting. She knew herself. She appreciated her talents and she shared them with others.

When I left Delaware the next summer, Marguerite called me to her house and gave me tokens of her friendship and love. Rather than an expensive gift bought in a store and wrapped in pretty paper and ribbon, she gave me a part of her: paintings of Delaware fall foliage and a summer beach scene; a small wired kerosene lamp that, as a child, she had nightly carried to her room. With each gift, she unraveled beautiful stories of its history. She gave me boxes of school materials that she had carefully organized during her teaching career.

I was young and my teaching career was just beginning; she was retiring to paint and enjoy her farm. We were best friends. The years between us was a blessing. I was the student and she was my teacher. She taught me as her students before. Through the years we stayed in touch and she continued to teach me about life. I visited her many times and she would visit me. Each visit was a lesson in life and history; in attitude and understanding. Her life was full. Years later, when most are considering nursing homes, Marguerite sold her farm to her grandson and bought a house on the historic register, carefully restoring it to its original beauty. Each room was filled with her warmth and charm.

The last summer I visited Marguerite was as exciting as the first. I took my 12-year-old son with me and he marveled at her stories as I had done years before. She made him crab cakes and she talked of American history and her life. We walked to town and ate ice cream at the drug store. She gave him a painting of a clam digger and told the story in such detail that he treasures the canvas as a friend. When we left, she stood on her porch and waved to us as she had done so many times before. We never saw her again.

POETRY

The Delta

Back from the rolling pastures green,
   The rich fertile soil that is not seen
Beneath the rows so neat and laid
   By a tractor's plow and farmer's spade.

Down from the house; up from the creek,
   The big old barn where the workers meet
To discuss the day's events and crops,
   To praise the sun and cuss the raindrops.

Away from the hustle and bustle of life
   To this place where things of strife
Are examples of patience, loyalty, and trust,
   Where beautiful cotton was once but dust.

The Lonely Steeple

The old church steeple is bent with age
     Torn by members not worshipping there.
Steps are gone, the windows boarded,
     People do not visit or care.
Hymnal pages, yellowed with age,
     Scatter upon the floor.
A bird's nest peeks from rotting rafters;
     The knob is gone from the door.
Wildflowers push their way inside
     And the pews are not there any more.
The yard is covered with sticks and litter,
     And weeds hide the sidewalk's stones.
But the old man can hear the sermon's fire
     And the faithful parishioners' moans.
Like the faithful few he was grayed and old;
     He had no choice but to go.
The congregation left this place,
     The country church they loved so.
But as they pass, they never stop
     To give their presence or sound.
Soon, out of loneliness and disrepair
     The church fell to the ground.
Its ruins stand to mark the spot
     Where laughter and spirits soared.
But progress and complacency took their toll;
     People often abandon what they adored.
The walls hold memories of baptisms, a marriage,
     The christening of their child.

He stands before the once-sacred altar
  And prays his prayer out loud.

"Where is the laughter? Where is the sound
  of happy running feet?
Of years of caring, loving friends
  Desiring a chance to meet?
Oh, Lord, let someone care for you
  More than they cared for this place,
And let my days of preaching here
  Make a difference in life's race."

His Spring of Life

Spring of Life; how hushed and quiet
    He didn't want her to die.
He heard her name; memories recalled
    Tempting him to cry.

Suppressed desire: leave him alone
    Haunting the day and night
Leave! Go to another poor soul.
    Let him decide wrong from right.

Spring of Life; He met her again.
    Her presence was ever near.
But looking into the depth of his heart
    He knew her place was not here.

Oh, Death is mean; ever cruel
    But Life is sometimes worse.
To live but want to die from pain
    Is there a greater curse?

She made a place among the strange
    In a land she did not own.
She found smiles and many friends
    But within, she felt alone.

This Spring of Life was leaving him
    She'd filled her years to the brim
With fun and laugher, tears and sorrow
    But her memory was growing dim.

He wanted her to live a day or two
    A week, a month or even a year.
Each night he'd sit by her bedside.
    He wanted to be near.

Spring of Life; come back to him
    He'll never fear what he can see.
But now he must meet with her
    In the depths of lasting memory.

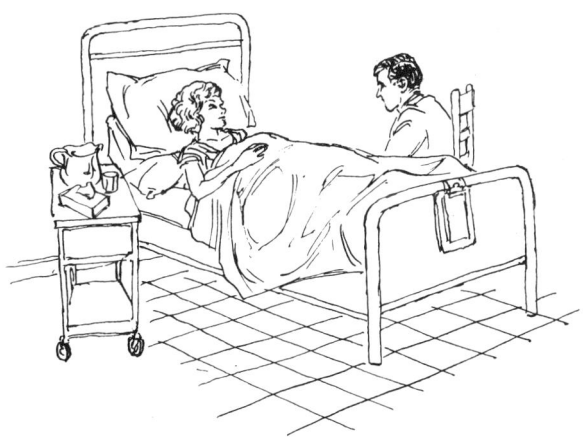

I Watched My Child
Fall Asleep Tonight

I watched my child fall asleep tonight.
    His eyelids slowly fell and he drifted into peace.
His words were simple—his last and only care:
    "When will I be four?"

I watched my child fall asleep tonight.
    His face showed the tiredness of a day's play.
His lips quivered remembering his busy daily rounds.
    He had so much to do.

I watched my child fall asleep tonight.
    I held him in my arms to soothe an ache.
He looked at me with eyes so sure and big.
    What can I say to him?

I watched my child fall asleep tonight.
    He looks so secure and awed by sleep.
He has no care; no worry for his future.
    His world so very small.

I watched my child fall asleep tonight.
  What a joy to hold his body of perfection.
The prayers are there; unsaid but in my heart.
  Be happy always—child of mine.

Final Requiem

You ask me if it's wrong to fear the day.
Must laughter share the present with inner tears?
Would it be Utopia if all life's chaos were erased?
Replaced by blissful smiles and happy years.

Why can't we live in happy dreams of beauty?
Why can't we be assured that love is a devoted mate?
Why can't happy tranquil thoughts dance within us?
Why can't there be an end to dissolution and hate?

If we were given endless patience for our fancy.
If within our eyes were only signs of hope.
If tears were for life, and only life existed.
And we were assured a chance to reconcile and cope.

Then we'd have more than an ounce of faith
Within our withered face of lifelong sin.
Yes, it would be simple if we had the answers
And could see eternity instead of trusting Him.

A Fallen Flower

Exploring Nature's gardens in the spring
Startled to find on the trodden path
A fallen flower upon the ground
Alone—perhaps from a human's wrath.

As I caressed the petals, soft and frail,
I wondered why someone threw it there.
Who had picked it for its beauty
But thrown it away and showed no care?

Its flower friends were in fullest bloom.
They seemed to mourn their brother's fate.
That poor lost flower of early spring
Was it a victim of unintentional hate?

I buried it in the coolness of the creek
And in the petals, I clearly saw human life—
Our years of doubting, needing, searching,
Many lives filled with endless strife.

We need nourishment in our youthful years
Just as the flower needed the rain and sun.
One difference—we have people who love
But the flower had died; it has none.

Most parents give love and tender care
But teachers must show concern every day
Because some students, like the fallen flower,
Are born, but thrown away.

He Could Not Speak His Love

He didn't say he loved him; it was understood.
To express feelings, for him was very hard.
He would not write poetry, even if he could;
He never even offered him a sentimental card.

He still insisted that his love was deep
And that the silence meant more than other men.
He argued that the best thoughts are those we keep,
Believing that men sharing inner feelings was a sin.

He felt in sharing life, they knew their part.
He felt they didn't need to reassure each other.
He knew inside how he felt within his heart;
He was more to him than just his father.

Standing by him when others turned away.
Believing in his dreams when they were dim.
The father had been there for him every day;
The young man had never doubted him.

The son has realized his greatest ambition.
Today, he is doing what he knows he can.
Fortune and fame is a realized fruition.
Now, he doesn't need his father's hand.

The old man calls and talks to a machine.
He knows he has nothing to offer or give.
He waits for his doorbell or phone to ring.
He has only a few more years to live.

He talks to friends with proud acclaim.
His son is everything he wanted him to be.
He says to the grandson that shares his name,
"All I want is for him to say he loves me."

Little Baby, Please Don't Cry

The young girl screamed,

"Little baby on the floor, don't you cry any more.
Mother's here but Daddy's gone.
He won't be back until the dawn.
He'll drink and drink at the nearest bar.
He'll get all drunk and wreck our car.

There'll be no more going; no more seeing
Of this worthless human being.
It is your Father that will do all this.
We once shared a home filled with bliss
But he wrecked it all and went astray
With a different woman every day.

Little baby on the floor, if you cry any more
I won't shout nor will I scold,
I'll just leave you in the cold.
I hate to do it, but you see
There's nothing left for you or me.
Daddy's gone and he won't see you on the floor.

Maybe he's in Heaven; maybe not.
Couldn't he see that I cared a lot?
If he only had loved me
Oh the changes there would be
But now he's gone and it's just me
A good mom I'll be to you
Maybe find us another Daddy, too."

Preserving Our Heritage

I looked upon a beautiful forest.
    Long did I scan its scope.
But nothing could I see in it.
    And in the scene, found no hope.

The trees were cut and in their place
    Ashes and broken branches stood.
Homeless birds circled overhead,
    Finding refuge as best they could.

The trucks are filled with the logs,
    Products of the trees they kill.
No time to waste; they have to leave,
    To make it to the paper mill.

"We have so many natural forests
    There's enough for everyone."
On they roll over beautiful country
    Until the clearing is all done.

So who will speak for Nature?
    Who will hear her sigh?
Will you give up your lifestyle,
    So the forest will not die?

One lone voice, though not enough
    May inspire other lips' release
So look upon the forest once again
    And do your part to bring it peace.

A Runner's Rage

The storm rages like her heartbeat.
The trees bend like a tired aching body.
A bolt of lightning flashes in her eyes.
It's dark, but light and sky play tricks.
The wind pushes back her hair as she runs,
Cold mist strikes roughly on her cheeks.
Is that the rustle of falling limbs?
She wonders where the message hides.
The storm continues as she struggles.
Obstacles of debris line city streets.

The wind subsides; her fears released.
Flowers beaten down, begin to stiffen.
Storm-kissed rain shimmers on a leaf.
Stillness plagues her inner thoughts.
Once the raging indecision; now the confidence.
What inner peace she feels and calls her own.
It's the runner's world she loves.

Rendezvous

The stillness, the quiet gentle tranquility
Our shore of drifting sand
Placid waves; designs of seaweed,
Sacrifices to our feet.
Gulls converge and wing the wind;
Tarnished shells lie still below
Hull, rich in strength
Beckons to the mast.
Alone, the two of us raise the anchor
The craft skimmers like a cloud.
Gone!

Foreign Faces

They were young, yet old and smelly,
With dirty fingernails and greasy hair.
They came hungry and some were shoeless,
But everyone was welcome there.

We watched though guarded and unsure,
Each threatened by a look or touch.
Afraid to answer any nod or smile,
But wanting to give so much.

This mission was their refuge.
The stew was needed nourishment.
Our job was serving food and child care.
That's why that we'd be sent.

Each morning empty eyes and stomachs,
Huddled begging for our care.
As the mission doors were opened,
There were a hundred waiting there.

They asked why we came to help them.
We couldn't answer truthfully.
Our thoughts had been so pious,
With our middle class integrity.

A week of stew we gave away,
While hearing tales of homeless men.
We encouraged women and the children,
And wondered where they had been.

Though we should have learned it sooner,
It was clear after just a short week
The message of the Lord's Kingdom,
Is more than what you speak.

Sacred Shrine

Stained glass windows
Organ music
Robed choir voices
Lighted candles
Quiet worship

A narthex of greeting
Claimed pews of polished wood
A lectern of notes
Times of laughter
Noisy fellowship

Here we baptize
Marry and bury
A communion of friends
Memories shared

Memories Of The Sixties

There's a new craze coming to the school
It's taken the students body and soul
It's the best invention since the Kiss
We all are calling it the "Schoolday Twist."

So let your hair down, girls
Come on and iron out the curls
Meet me tonight in the old band hall
Man, we will really have a ball.

Turn the record up loud as it will go
Limber up and twist yourself so
I've got the rhythm in my head
I shan't be happy till the twist I've led.

Couples, get together, two by two
We all know what's come over you
Misters, grab your little Miss
Go down the hall doing the twist.

When we twist until we're sore
We'll still go on and do it more
It's got us going; it's good to do
Grab me, baby, I gotta twist with you.

We've got it bad; so don't be late
Be in the hall at half past eight
This school will really rock tonight
When we twist with all our might.

Let the square ones talk; we won't care
Forget them, Honey, and meet me there
You be my partner; I'll be your Miss
Cause tonight, Sweetheart, we gonna twist.

The Birthday Resolve

He was turning twelve in less than a month.
Bikes and toys should be his dream.
He wasn't interested in those things.
He had a more serious gift in his scheme.

"Do you want us to buy you that new bike?"
We'll add some money to the dollars you've saved."
No answer he gave; she feared the worst.
He couldn't have the motorscooter he craved.

"No, I want no bike. My old one is fine.
I want nothing from the stores in town.
What I want is something you cannot give.
I want you to lay your cigarettes down."

The Mother hugged her son so tight,
But she said nothing to assure the deed.
She'd tried to quit many times before.
She didn't want to swear and not succeed.

The tall young man looked at her with love.
Would that love be worth the pain?
He wanted a gift that money couldn't buy.
He said, "I'll never ask you again."

That night she sat in front of the fire.
She thought and smoked while he slept.
She took the package and threw it away.
It would be one promise that she kept.

For three long weeks, she didn't smoke.
Saying nothing, she took it day by day.
It would have been easier to buy the bike,
But she was determined to give him his way.

The day of his birthday she had kept her word.
She announced she was giving him his request.
He blew out his candles and opened presents.
But her gift was better than all the rest.

His smile of pride was worth the price.
He would help her any way he could.
"Just tell me you love me, that's all I want."
He promised he did and always would.

Thank You

Thank you
For not resisting
When I wanted to surprise you.

Thank you
For letting me
Plan a celebration of fun.

Thank you
For being willing
To accept the tricks and schemes.

Thank you
For holding my hand
And for sweetly telling me

Thank you